Why Do They Call It
BUSINESS

If It's Mostly
POLITICS ?

By: Mike Latimer

Why Do They Call It Business If It's Mostly Politics?

Copyright © 1999

The Truth Squad LLC

First Printing 1999
Universal Publishers/uPUBLISH.com
USA • 1999
ISBN: 1-58112-814-2
www.upublish.com/books/latimer.htm

Cover graphics by Nicole Swift
nickiswift@hotmail.com

Cover illustration by Doug Pike
www.doubtfulaccounts.com

While the events and persons portrayed in these accounts are real, all of the names, places and unique similarities to actual events have been modified to preserve their confidentiality

ii

Dedication

To my baby daughter Monica:

Being an author is fun.
Being your father is fantastic.

Acknowledgments

To my loving wife and partner Cindy
Whose remarkable way with words and animals helped make this book
possible.

To Tom Moore
Whose interest and encouragement helped get this project going.

To Dudley, Hayley, Elsa and Kosmo
Who kept me company while the project kept me busy.

To Doug Pike
Whose thoughtful advice and feedback helped keep things on track.

To Justin Hayward, John Lodge,
Ray Thomas, Graeme Edge and Mike Pinder
Whose creativity and innovative spirit
have been a constant source of inspiration
for me and millions of others

And to SteveN and FrankieDan
For reasons they will understand

iii

In Loving Memory

To my mother, Merrick Farrar Latimer

Her brother, the Rev. Charles Bidwell Farrar

TABLE OF CONTENTS

Introduction   1

Chapter 1- Test Your Knowledge   5

Chapter 2- When Worlds Apart, Collide   8

Chapter 3- Running with the Pack   13

    The Side-Show of Force   16
    The Feud Chain   16
    Usurp, U pay   18
    Truth Decay   20
    Facts Evasion   23
    The Math of Least Resistance   26
    Accost Accounting   28
    Bar-B-Q'd Bean Counters   28
    Blocking The Bottom-Line Backer   34
    Leggo My Ego   36
    The Self-Esteem Roller   38
    Chicken of the "C"   40
    Zero Worship   41
    The Glass Ceiling Fans   43
    Chapter Summary   44

Chapter 4- Conspiring in the Colony   49

    The Tunnel Vision-ary   51
    A Busyness Trip   53
    Business As Use-U-All   56
    Managing the Work Farce   57
    Welcome-Door Mat   57
    Working On the Weakened   59
    Duty-Free Gifts   59
    Naiveté Scene   61
    Winning by Wearing Down   62
    A Penance for Your Thoughts   64
    The Holey Roamin' Empire   65
    Delta Coup D'Etat   67
    The Road-Kill to Success   68
    Error Apparent   69
    Diplomatic Immunity   70
    Looking for Mr. Good Bargain   72
    Who's Undermining the Store?   75
    The Pocket Veto   77
    Excessive Wait Loss   79
    Chapter Summary   80

Chapter 5- Consorting with the Clan   85

Hush-Hush Sweet Charlatan   88
Quest For Fire-ing   91
Pretty in Pink-Slip   94
Pirates of Pensions   95
The High Price of Admission   97
Your Slip-Up is Showing   100
The Parent-Company Trap   101
The Way We War   103
Raging Bull _ _ _ _   105
How the Worst Was Won   109
Staff Infection   110
The Discredit Union   113
Talking on the Tell-A-Phony Line   116
It's True - Moral Less   117
Beyond A Reasonable Clout   118
Malice in WunderKind   119
The One-UpsmanShip-Wreck   121
The Shining   123
Chapter Summary   124

Chapter 6- Floating with the Pod   129

Conclusion- It's Time To Change Your Unaware   132

Afterword   146

INTRODUCTION

"Why *do* they call it business if it's mostly politics?"

It only seems fair that we answer that question before moving on to the rest of the story.

But before we do, we'd better begin by defining our terms so we're all speaking the same language.

Business is what people conduct in a system of enterprise to acquire valuable assets,

and

Politics is what people practice in a system of government to accomplish various agendas.

These two unrelated areas apparently have nothing in common, right?

Well, not quite.

Somehow these two managed to meet one another, get together and form a relationship. The ostensible purpose of this relationship was to help each other get ahead in the world. Their togetherness eventually spawned an offspring.

The offspring ended up becoming an oxymoron, and was named "corporate politics."

Not surprisingly, it has turned out to be very unwanted offspring. Neither of its procreators seems willing to claim it as their own.

On the business side of the family, it is true that corporate politics is occasionally featured in management books and articles.

However, the mentions that it gets are mostly couched in connotations and indirect references to "cultural barriers" in "no-consequence" companies headed by "non-accountable" leaders. This level of representation does not constitute outright acceptance of corporate politics as a legitimate offspring of the business world.

On the political side, things aren't much different. Despite an uncanny resemblance to this side of the family, the world of politics steadfastly refuses to accept any responsibility for it. You certainly won't find any mention of it in the Lawmakers Home Journal or Politicians Quarterly. As far as the real politicians are concerned, this offspring isn't one they have to live with - so it's simply not their problem.

That is why it's called business even though it's mostly politics. It has taken the name of the parent that has full custody.

Unfortunately for some, the living arrangements have proven to be a bit dysfunctional at times. It's probably because corporate politics has become quite an imposition since its conception. Those who live on the business side of the house have been frustrated by its propensity to interfere in their affairs. Despite all of the advancements that the business world has made intellectually and technologically, it has been unable to block out this interference.

The only way it can ever hope to block out the interference is to pinpoint its source. But in the case of corporate politics, the source of the interference is too deeply embedded in the immovable forces of nature.

Human nature, that is.

No matter how the business world tries to distance itself from it, there is no escaping its influence. Human nature, teeming with all of its virtuous strengths and petty weaknesses, ultimately drives the behavior of business organizations everywhere. Behind all of the triumphs and hardships that organizations experience, you can see its influence at work. It imbues each organization with its own unique personality, and brings along its own unique set of problems.

While it may be easier to blame the problems on a lack of strategy or management ability, it fails to acknowledge human nature as the epicenter of every behavior that occurs in organizations. Basic human behaviors are not automatically altered by a change in the environment. People always bring along their own unique way of looking at things when they move from the world outside of business to the one inside. They also bring along a variety of coping mechanisms, some of which are friendly and cooperative, and others which are not.

As the need to control the environment possesses some more than others, aggressive behavior ensues. Perceived threats in the environment cause people to react instinctively in ways that are often counterproductive to others elsewhere in the system. While all of this presumably takes place under the auspices of those in authority, most are powerless to prevent it from disrupting the organization.

Yet, in spite of all the evidence to the contrary, many businesspeople still choose to believe that the mere existence of a corporate charter will miraculously exorcise all non-comformist thoughts and behaviors from everyone who goes to work for an organization. In their way of thinking, when people share a common space and a common goal, they should gratuitously set aside any personal ideas or agendas that are contrary to those of the organization. However, when you strip away all of the pomp, circumstance and other trappings of corporate life, business is all about people with position and power over other people. In that regard, it is no different than government.

In government, people in authority are prone to behaviors that range anywhere from occasional indiscretions to extraordinary abuses of power. Yet many still cling to the notion that businesspeople should be immune to that sort of behavior. Such a notion ignores the basic fact that human nature is as powerful a force in the world of business as it is in politics. It engenders impulsive feelings and behaviors that people act upon when confronted with difficult or undesirable situations. When push comes to shove, these instincts can quickly stifle the inner voices calling out for reason and rational judgment.

In the world of business, there is evidence of this every day.

- An individual's quest for control impedes an organization's plans to go public. Growth stops.

- An individual's will to survive undercuts an organization's succession plan. Leadership weakens.

- An individual's fear of change undermines an organization's attempt to restructure. Profitability suffers.

The evidence is very difficult to ignore when your career, or the career of someone close to you, is adversely affected by those who indulge that sort of behavior. While no amount of preparation can be guaranteed foolproof, those who take the time to understand the forces behind it are those in the best position to either deal with it, overcome it, or even benefit from it.

By the time you finish reading this book, you will gain that much-needed awareness of the forces behind corporate politics. You will better understand how political behavior affects you and everyone else in your organization. You'll learn how to predict the consequences of that behavior and deal with them effectively. Most importantly, you'll understand what it takes to coexist peacefully with the ever-present political forces in your organization, while keeping yourself firmly ensconced in solid business practices.

Relax and enjoy! And be sure to visit the Afterword section at the end of the book to learn how you can share your own experiences.

4

CHAPTER 1 - TEST YOUR KNOWLEDGE

CAN YOU DISTINGUISH THE POLITICAL ANIMALS FROM THE REST OF THE CORPORATE WILDLIFE?

In order to gauge your level of familiarity and general understanding of corporate politics, please answer the following multiple choice questions. Select the one whose behavior is best described.

Question #1
They strike suddenly and without warning, injecting their poison and waiting patiently for it to render their victim helpless.

Are they?

1. Anacondas
2. Koala Bears
3. Vipers
4. Corporate Politicians

Question #2
They sneak up on and quickly grab their prey, gradually coiling around them and squeezing harder and harder until the victim's effort to resist has been extinguished.

Are they?

1. Earthworms
2. Boa Constrictors
3. Eels
4. Corporate Politicians

Question #3

They pursue their prey relentlessly until it becomes completely worn down and totally vulnerable. They then inflict a series of small injuries on the prey until it is so weakened that it can be easily killed and dismembered.

Are they?

1. Wolves
2. Coyotes
3. MeerKats
4. Corporate Politicians

Question #4

They have an annoying tendency to assault their slower moving, more benign counterparts by attacking in large numbers and overpowering even the most giant of prey.

Are they?

1. Dolphins
2. Killer Whales
3. Red Snappers
4. Corporate Politicians

Question #5

They are the first to spot dead meat. Nothing can strip a carcass down to the bare bones any faster. The tell-tale circling of their kind is foolproof evidence that some poor beast has met its end.

Are they?

1. Pink Flamingos
2. African Ostriches
3. Egyptian Vultures
4. Corporate Politicians

Question #6

Although spineless, these remarkable creatures possess considerable intelligence. Taking advantage of their far-reaching tentacles and a lot of suckers, they draw their struggling prey ever closer to their voracious orifice.

Are they?

1. Red Lobsters
2. Giant Squid
3. Sea Anemones
4. Corporate Politicians

Answer Guide

If you answered #4 to all of the above questions, you are quite conversant with the topic of corporate politics.

If your answers were 3,2,1,2,2,3 then you need to turn off the Nature Channel and read this book as quickly as possible.

CHAPTER 2

WHEN WORLDS APART, COLLIDE

You've heard that politics and religion don't mix. Well unfortunately, the same is not true for politics and business. They do mix, and when they do, they make very strange bedfellows.

Corporate politics is the result of a head-on collision between two worlds that, in the purest sense, are at complete odds with each other. It is very rare to find a business organization that is purely business-oriented or purely political. The two worlds have been intertwined for so long that it's difficult to know where one starts and the other ends. To gain an understanding of how the combination of these two worlds can complicate the business careers of so many people, we must begin by examining them separately. Seeing them in their purest form will help us understand how they're supposed to function when they aren't hopelessly commingled.

Let's start with the business world.

In a world that is purely business, everything revolves around getting more and more results year after year. It is a very systematic process that is typically focused on the customer.

The business process usually involves:

1. Identifying opportunities to create value.
2. Setting specific goals and objectives (with deadlines).
3. Assigning responsibility for achieving those goals and objectives.
4. Measuring performance against those goals and objectives.
5. Rewarding those who achieve them and replacing those who don't.

In a world that is purely political, everything revolves around those who are in power. It's not about delivering more and better each year. It's about keeping things on an even keel. The process, which is highly systemic in nature, is focused on satisfying a constituency.

The political process generally involves:

1. Influencing public opinion.
2. Imposing checks and balances.
3. Legislating policies and programs that elevate the status quo.
4. Expanding the government's span of control at home.
5. Extending the government's sphere of influence abroad.

You can clearly see a world of opposites when you compare them this way:

	World of Business	World of Politics
The end goal is to increase	Value	Influence
By instituting	Goals & Objectives	Checks & Balances
And managing	Performance	Perceptions
To satisfy	Customers	Constituents
And get	Results	Returns

Apart from each other, these worlds are actually quite productive. When these two worlds intertwine, dysfunctional and destructive behavior can ensue.

So how did the two get mixed up with each other in the first place?

There is a great deal of history behind that. Elements from the public and private sector have been joined at the hip since the birth of the Industrial Age in America. The onset of two world wars, followed by the cold war, required a joint effort from both the public and private sectors in order to ensure the United States' survival as a nation. During this period, many of our country's major industrial and commercial enterprises adopted management structures and practices from the public sector. What was adopted was a very "command and control" oriented approach to business management. The corporate bureaucracy, with its extremely mechanical ensemble of departments and divisions, was the (step)child of this wartime marriage of the public and private sector.

Over the last twenty years or so, much of the collective energy expended in the business world has been aimed at trying to unravel the bureaucracy that still exists in a lot of companies. But this pulling apart of the bureaucracy has not managed to separate the political elements from the business elements in the private sector. These political elements have been afforded more than enough time to adapt themselves to the corporate world. It has now become quite a natural habitat for them. Today there is no such thing as an organization completely devoid of politics. Every organization shows some signs of it. The only real question is, "Is it the dominant life form?"

If politics happens to be the dominant life form, everyone in the organization must subordinate their behavior to the dominant species. Their only choice is to adapt or become extinct.

If politics is not the dominant life form, business-as-usual will rule the day.

Most organizations find themselves somewhere between these two extremes. In these organizations, the behavior is not altogether focused on business or politics. The business and political elements coexist and battle each other for supremacy. The behavior is not unlike what you'd witness in the animal kingdom. That's because in all but a few of the species of animals that work together to survive, life revolves around the pecking order. In their quest to control this pecking order, you find ordinary human beings exhibiting animal-like tendencies in their struggle to make some organization their eminent domain. It is this sort of animal-like behavior that defines the nature of the relationship between an organization's leaders and followers. It can either be hostile or harmonious. People can work with each other or against each other. The nature of this relationship also determines the nature of the politics involved. If the relationship is adversarial, then the politics will most likely be brutal.

This sort of interaction is germane to the animal kingdom. In this parallel world unfettered by the trappings of corporate life, the members of each animal group instinctively act out their aggressions or affections without concern for its effect on others. According to Maslow's hierarchy of needs, animals in the wild are rarely preoccupied about anything beyond their need to survive. Humans in the corporate world, on the other hand, have needs that extend all the way to the top of the hierarchy. Many feel compelled to satisfy those needs through a series of self-actualizing behaviors. Once you understand the rationale behind these compulsive behaviors, you can better understand the nature of the politics involved.

In the animal kingdom, four of the basic groups of animals that live and work together are known as Packs, Pods, Colonies and Clans. Each has its own variety of species. What makes these groups so unique is the way they interact amongst themselves. Except for a few basic similarities, each has their own fundamentally distinct code of conduct that governs how the leaders and followers behave towards each other. These codes of conduct are not unlike the patterns of behavior that people exhibit in organizations. The similarities are so obvious that one can actually predict behavior once you know where the people in your organization fit within each group.

It is quite possible, even probable, that more than one group can exist in an organization at the same time. Sometimes, different people in different departments in different divisions of the same company can each exhibit one or more of these unique patterns of behavior. Having conditioned their followers to respond to their own particular code of conduct, these leaders effectively establish their own separate domains. Until you know where their boundaries are, and where the lines are drawn, you will find it nearly impossible to peacefully co-exist with them and successfully navigate (or circumnavigate) the labyrinth that they have laid before you.

Our foray into the mysterious world of corporate politics begins with a look at its more pugnacious variety - the Pack.

CHAPTER 3 - RUNNING WITH THE PACK

"We keep you alive to serve this ship. Row well...and live."

Jack Hawkins as Quintus Arius
from the movie <u>Ben-Hur</u>

Animals that live and work together in packs are subject to some of the strictest rules and rulemakers that you'll find anywhere in the animal kingdom.

Led by a dominant male and his mate, the higher-ups in the pecking order usually consist of the leader's offspring. Beyond this immediate entourage, everyone else is subordinate and considered inferior. It is an accepted practice for the dominant few to intimidate subordinates and prevent them from having relations to strengthen their numbers.

Everyone in the pack lives to take care of the higher-ups. In return, the pack members receive group benefits, namely the chance to feed on the prey that the pack manages to kill. For those choosing to act as "lone wolves", there are only rodents and other inauspicious prey to pursue. Therefore, they stay together to benefit from safety in numbers, even if it means catering to the needs of the dominant few.

In cases where a dominant member decides that a subordinate needs to be put in his place, he automatically bares his fangs, growls ferociously, and may even reach for the offender's scruff. The lesser creature must then show submission by quickly rolling over, exposing his vulnerable under-belly, whining, and then licking his superior's chops to make restitution. Further acts of defiance by an inferior can result in his, or her, being driven from the pack.

In the corporate world, you're part of a pack if you find yourself surrounded by oppressive leaders who exhibit this sort of behavior, and submissive followers who reluctantly endure it.

The pack mentality in a business organization takes on quite a few not-so-desirable characteristics. Among them are:

Leaders who treat followers as inferiors
Leaders who use intimidation to keep followers under control
Followers who are afraid of their leader(s).
Followers who grudgingly accept abuse from them.

If an organization finds itself in this state of nature, the battle for supremacy between the political and business people can be very hard on those caught in the crossfire. Unlike the other corporate landscapes we will traverse, this one is incredibly difficult to navigate, no matter who is in control. While intimidation can be used by both business and political types to suit their purpose, the specific applications are considerably different.

When business-minded people resort to intimidation, the needs of the business take precedence over those of the rank and file. Employees are expected to follow some incredibly hard and extremely fast rules of business:

Do and say nothing until you have the facts to back it up.

Solve problems immediately, not when you get around to them

Meet deadlines; Never move them.

Underpromise; Overperform

The career-limiting penalties for failure in this environment include a total and potentially irredeemable loss of credibility. The single most dreaded penalty is denial of future access to the upper echelons in the organization.

On the surface, it all seems incredibly unfair to those who have to cope with it. The question it begs is, Is there anyone who benefits from running at this fast and furious pace?

The answer is yes, and there are five groups to choose from.

a) The leaders of the organization (executives)
b) The followers in the organization (employees)
c) The owners of the organization (shareholders)
d) The stakeholders in the organization (lenders, vendors, etc.)
e) The patrons of the organization (customers)

If the answer to the question is (c), (d) and (e), the people in group (a) are running the organization like a business. People often forget the importance of these three groups, whose resources make it possible for the organization to stay in business. When occasionally overbearing methods are used to run the business a little harder or a little faster, the people in category (b) have to take some comfort in the knowledge that their sacrifices ultimately benefit those who will sustain the life of their organization.

If the answer to the question is (a) and only (a), then you can safely assume that at some point in the history of the organization, the political forces managed to gain the upper hand and wield it for their own personal gain. If these political forces have a pack mentality, they will resort to any means necessary to protect their position in the power structure. The most frequently used tactic is a very sinister form of intimidation that strikes at those who make any attempt to think or act independently. It doesn't matter if the thought or action might benefit someone in group (b), (c), (d) or (e). If there is even the remotest possibility that it could potentially undermine the authority of the powers-that-be, it will summon as its main attraction a horrific display of power politics, followed by a not-so-entertaining...

SIDE-SHOW OF FORCE

When leaders in an organization shift their focus away from working the business towards the playing of politics, they tend to be easily angered by anything that resembles a loss of control over the people and property within their purview. Any threat, no matter how small or insignificant, automatically triggers a ballistic form of behavior aimed at pulverizing the target and paralyzing its ability to respond or undertake any further "threatening" actions in the future. In most cases, the issues are really quite trivial and almost totally unrelated to the real day-to-day business of the organization. Sometimes, something as simple as the agenda for a meeting or the cc's on a memo can provoke this kind of attack. By regularly demonstrating their lack of hesitation to launch a pre-emptive strike against anyone for any reason, they effectively divert people's attention away from attacking the real issues in the business. They keep everybody preoccupied with keeping the peace on side issues that have no real impact on the performance of the organization.

Many of the people who get sidetracked by these shows of force never figure out what knocked them off course. One minute they're engineering a major new product and the next minute they're relegated to mopping up loose ends on some low-budget project whose priority was never very high to begin with.

They're the ones who find themselves getting jerked around at the end of...

THE FEUD CHAIN

The people who inevitably get throttled in this situation are the ones who mistakenly believe that their survival in the organization is solely a function of their performance. They continue to act as though the business forces were in control. They go about their business of finding problems and trying to solve them overnight. They tend to ignore the fact that a politically-minded regime might be more interested in protecting the status quo. The minute a performance-oriented

16

organization person (p.o.o.p.) lands in their political punch-bowl, the party's over.

Take the case of Arthur. Arthur was a division controller who worked for a large real estate company. One day, Arthur found himself put in charge of tracking the performance of a major division of the company - the Relocation Services Division. The performance of this division had never been tracked by anyone. The business had traditionally been conducted on a best-efforts basis. The department head responsible for overseeing its activities suddenly became concerned about this second set of eyes peering into his sphere of influence.

Of course Arthur was delighted by this assignment. He saw it as a welcome vote of confidence that he needed to move up in the organization. He therefore took his new assignment to heart, confident that he could uncover the secrets to improved performance in the Relocation Division. He began by reviewing the costs associated with buying, holding and selling the homes of client company employees who were relocating. This was, after all, the largest and most expensive activity in the entire division. Arthur was sure he could find some way to improve this function and reduce its costs.

Unfortunately for Arthur, he didn't realize that the department head of the Relocation Division was the kind of person who had absolutely no tolerance for scavengers rummaging through his backyard. To him, it didn't matter that Arthur was collaborating with members of his own staff. He believed that Arthur was out to prove that his department hadn't been run as well as it should have been. For that, he needed to be taught a lesson and put in his place.

When the time came to present Arthur's performance report, Arthur's boss, the department head of the Relocation Division and his staff were there to review the findings. Arthur proudly presented his finding that the division's performance was being incorrectly stated due to the

17

manner in which the inventory of homes was being counted. According to him, the company was still incurring costs on inventory that had previously been recorded as sold.

What happened next resembled a sordid twist on a popular Disney film. In a manner reminiscent of Cruella de Ville, the head of the Relocation Division proceeded to turn loose a savage attack of

101 Damnations

His foray into the four letter world went so far as to double the X-rated vocabulary of everyone in the room.

Despite the merits of his arguments, Arthur was blown away by the winds of fury that he unexpectedly unleashed upon himself and his boss. In order to salvage the situation, Arthur's boss was forced to roll over on the issue. The defeat was chalked up to Arthur's apparent lack of diplomacy in dealing with higher ups in the organization. All that Arthur could do was beat an infamous retreat back to sanctuary - and obscurity.

Arthur's debacle sent a message to all of the other p.o.o.p.'s floating around the organization. The message, which dangled ominously from the heavy metal chain of command, read:

USURP, U PAY

In other words, if you ever get caught trying to pull a politician's platform out from under them, you will find yourself in one of two very awkward situations - either bent over, or on your knees. In these rather vulnerable positions, an experienced politician can make sure you live to regret it for a very long time.

Anyone brave enough to question the goings-on in a politico's business should first heed the following storm warning that will promptly enter their immediate forecast:

Flashes of lying
Plenty of stolen thunder
Lots of hard-blowing wind

The remarkably furious backlash that can be triggered by the slightest hint of criticism is a very definite sign that things have turned political. To defend their coveted position of unquestionable power and authority, politicians must do everything in their power to keep any chinks from appearing in their armor. For these leaders, maintaining the perception that they have everything in hand and on track is absolutely critical to their success.

Maintaining this perception is particularly paramount when performance starts to deteriorate.

In an organization governed by business principles, a slippage in performance is typically followed by some form of failure analysis to find the problems and fix them. In an organization governed by political principles, failure analysis is usually put off as too risky. If the analysis were to uncover a problem, it might precipitate a major change. The change could alter the corporate landscape and upset the balance of power. Therefore, those at risk of being found out are always sure to observe the first hard and fast rule of politics which states:

"Don't ever take a chance if there's a chance you might be wrong"

The result of this sort of reasoning is inertia. Without any form of failure analysis, an organization has no way of knowing if it's being run the wrong way. As more time passes in this state of inertia, another more troublesome form of behavior sets in.

Rationalization.

In most business situations, this word means the organization has fumbled the ball away and switched from offense to defense. Everything is now viewed against the backdrop of recent performance. Whatever happened a few months ago becomes the new benchmark. This approach honors the second hard and fast rule of politics which states:

"The past is prologue"

In other words, the quantity and quality of past performance now becomes the new standard for future performance. Therefore, no further changes are deemed necessary. The downturn in performance is either rationalized as temporary or attributed to forces outside the organization's immediate control.

In reality, it may be that the organization is seriously off track in some area of its business. It may be that a more radical change is required due to some major change in the industry, the competition, or the marketplace in general. Without change, there is nothing left but a systematic defense of past behaviors that have essentially outlived their usefulness. This refusal to brush with the forces of change inevitably leads to

TRUTH DECAY

There are people in the world who are capable of bending objects using the concentrated power of their brain waves.

There are politicians in the business world who can bend reality with a passing thought.

While it's true that everyone bends the truth a little from time to time, politicians have perfected it into a fine art form. They know how to paint an abstract picture of reality whenever the situation demands. Nowhere is this more apparent than report writing.

In organizations where the achievement of results is the sole motivation of management, it is generally an accepted practice to fully disclose in the management reports why the business did or did not perform well during the period. This full disclosure is supposed to explain what the organization is doing right, and what it is doing wrong. The purpose for doing so is to assure top management that the organization is effectively policing itself and owning up to its mistakes. When a mistake is identified and readily admitted, management's credibility may actually improve if it can explain how it intends to fix the problem(s).

This sort of intellectual honesty only works as long as the leaders of an organization expect it and respect it. If the discipline of full disclosure is ever interrupted for some reason, problems begin festering in the background. After a while, no one associated with a particular problem wants to admit that they knew about it and didn't fix it immediately. Before you know it, there aren't any more problems being mentioned in the management reports.

In business, this is popularly known as B.S.

However, the fact that it is B.S. doesn't stop the leaders of the organization from convincing themselves that their business is problem-free.

This is known as "Believing your own B.S."

Eventually, the absence of any meaningful discussion about business problems and solutions evolves into a meaningless monologue of self-congratulatory statements in the management reports.

At this point, the business has moved beyond the "Believing your own B.S." stage to the terminal stage - known as "Cheerleading your own B.S."

To give you some idea of just how contagious this condition can be, take the case of Ralph. Ralph was the distribution manager for a company that sold home appliances. His job was to establish distribution agreements with major retailers of consumer products. The ultimate objective for the company was to establish long term agreements with at least one of the three largest retailers in their category. These agreements would provide the company with the outlets it needed to distribute its product at less cost. It would also provide them with a springboard for launching new products and acquiring more customers.

That was how it was supposed to work on paper.

What actually happened was altogether different. Soon after his first attempts to procure the larger retailers turned up empty, Ralph knew he needed to quickly put up some numbers in order to protect his position in the company. Ralph decided to detour from the main objective and instead amass a horde of distribution agreements with smaller and lesser known companies whose scope of operations and market share were nowhere near the extent necessary to sustain a profitable relationship.

As time went by, these agreements began to fizzle out one by one, and Ralph had to keep adding on more of them to keep the illusion of success alive. His monthly management reports gave no hint of any problems with his approach, even though things had already started to unravel. Every month, Ralph paraded higher and higher numbers in front of everyone to prove how successful his endeavors were. Those who dared to question him were met with harsh criticism for being unsupportive of his unique approach to the program.

It took the company nearly two years to figure out what had happened. During Ralph's campaign to compile a portfolio of smaller retailers, new competitors were able to enter the market and secure distribution agreements with all of the major retailers. Ralph's program eventually collapsed under the combined weight of dozens of highly-unprofitable distribution agreements, resulting in a 30% loss of market share.

Ralph's story is an all-too-familiar account of what happens when people in management fall in love with their own ideas. Blinded by desire, people become overly protective of their "brain-children." They say or do whatever is necessary to convince themselves and everyone else around them that their ideas have merit. If anyone takes issue with their ideas, they take it personally. Eventually, every idea becomes an issue of personalities rather than performance. After a while, it starts becoming difficult to tell whether their substance is the stuff of politics or business. Whether the substance is business or political in nature depends upon the desired outcome.

In business, the desired outcome is gaining some new insight into the business that can be used to change it for the better.

In politics, the desired outcome is ratification of an existing position.

It doesn't matter how tenuous the position is, or how questionable the methods used to justify it. More often than not, the desired outcome is pre-determined. It precludes change by avoiding or ignoring the discovery of new information. In its most benign form, this approach involves nothing more than a harmless oversight of some minor details. In its more malignant form, it involves the deliberate withholding of information that might change a decision. This is known as...

FACTS EVASION

It is very easy to manipulate results when they are not measured properly. Without accurate measurement of an organization's performance, none of the decisions made by management can be authenticated. Everything that management does ends up being based on faith instead of fact.

This sort of environment is very conducive to politically motivated behavior. This behavior is particularly apparent in organizations controlled exclusively by a domineering group of like-minded individuals. These individuals may have been instrumental in the early design and development of the organization. They are typically the ones crediting themselves with helping the company achieve its current position in the industry.

They are also the ones most interested in protecting that position, and doing whatever is necessary to defend their past and future agenda for the organization. Whenever this agenda for the leadership is challenged by some unexpected turn of events in the business, some very interesting thinking gets unleashed.

Donald was just one of the people who experienced this dizzying display of logic when his company faced a significant dip in consumer response to its advertising program. For years, Donald's company had labored under the assumption that one advertising campaign could be deployed anywhere in the U.S. and that the only real threat to it was the level of advertising from competitors.

Donald did not share this way of thinking. He believed that the amount and the type of advertising employed in each market needed to vary depending on the demographics of the population and other unique characteristics.

When at one point the organization was faced with a sudden and unexpected drop in the response to its advertising, the company's management promptly fell back on its old school of thinking. They automatically assumed that a major influx of new competitors and competitive advertising must have somehow undermined the effectiveness of their own marketing efforts. The off-the-cuff solution to the problem was an immediate across-the-board increase in the level of spending - one that would retaliate against the competition and recapture the share of market that was being lost. This approach, which had been used extensively in the past to protect market share, was considered the first and only truly effective response to the actions of competitors.

The president promptly requested that the marketing department compile a short-order study of competitor advertising spending in defense of their position on the issue.

Although he was in less of a position to speak authoritatively, Donald suggested that any final conclusions on this issue be deferred until some research was done to determine whether any other factors were responsible for the downturn in response. He volunteered his staff to look at some of the variances on a market-by-market basis. What he uncovered was the fact that little if any of the problem was due to competitive factors. As it turned out, the company had previously agreed to let its advertising agency shift money between different media. This shift had inadvertently diminished the company's share of voice in the marketplace.

As a result of Donald's voluntary research effort, the company's media spending program had to be completely revamped to prevent further shortfalls in marketing from being self-inflicted on the organization.

"Oh What a Tangled Web We Weave".......

Facts evasion is a very debilitating condition in a business organization. The condition develops at the point where learning stops and speculation takes over. It takes its heaviest toll on those in the organization who are responsible for measuring and evaluating its performance. I'm talking about the inhabitants of your typical finance department, namely the financial accountants, auditors, planners and analysts. In most business environments, these people are charged with uncovering weaknesses in the company's operations and fixing problems with the company's finances. They are usually joined in this effort by other technical types in the organization, namely the engineers and computer specialists.

Their view of the business world is largely influenced by their study of the "Exact Sciences", otherwise known as Information Technology, Statistics, Engineering, Accounting, Finance, etc. These people are taught to believe that there is a slot for every tab and a formula to explain every behavior.

To them, if it can't be measured, it can't be managed.

By virtue of this highly scientific sort of upbringing, they tend to clash with the political elements in the organization who don't like having their results examined all that closely. When finance gets too close for comfort, a true politician will never wait to react. They go on the attack. Surprise attacks have a way of knocking their opponents in finance off track. It forces them to choose

THE MATH OF LEAST RESISTANCE

In every management report that never got to the bottom line, in every financial analysis that failed to find a weakness, and in every business plan that promised more than it delivered, you will find traces of the math of least resistance.

Finance people are frequently asked by those with something to hide to "interpret" certain events or transactions in such a way as to make them appear less threatening to them. This is not to suggest that they condone sloppy accounting practices. The politicians simply want an interpretation of the accounting that endorses their business practices. Their counterparts in finance know that it's not just a matter of keeping score - it's keeping up with those who have scores to settle. If the politics are governed by a pack mentality, the constant threat of retaliation can have a very intimidating effect on their judgment in any number of situations:

It can affect the way a financial analyst interprets a rise in the customer churn rate.

It can affect the way a systems analyst interprets a series of system failures.

It can affect the way a company controller interprets a pattern of escalating costs.

It can affect the way a business planner forecasts a downward trend in profitability.

These situations can transform otherwise objective people into spin doctors. Before they will reveal a weakness in the way the business is functioning, they will first find out if it is due to someone's long-standing neglect. If it involves a political leader who might be exposed as the culprit, their reluctance to make that knowledge public increases exponentially.

The last thing the numbers people want to have ringing in their ears is the corporate politicians' dreaded finance department cursery rhyme:

> Placate, Placate Finance Man
> Fake me some numbers as fast as you can
> Round 'em up, Roll 'em up
> Throw 'em in the Plan

Because a politically motivated leader's number one goal is to manage the perceptions that people have about their performance, they will resort to any means necessary to accomplish it. While they appear willing to delegate the responsibility for the accounting and analysis to others, they never relinquish the power to interpret it themselves. Their ultimate aim is to impose their own interpretation of events onto others in the organization. Since the finance and accounting people are taught to be suspicious of anyone who tries to interpret events for them, they become quite uncomfortable when someone tries to do just that.

27

Finance types do not relish confrontation with the leaders of their organization. Instead they prefer to argue the merits of their case in the hope that logic will ultimately prevail. This style of management leaves them grossly unprepared to deal with pack leaders who resort to intimidation whenever necessary to make their point and advance their position in the company.

Whenever politicos feel threatened with the loss of power by the forces of finance, they will apply their own generally acceptable accounting practices, collectively known as

ACCOST ACCOUNTING

Usually all it takes is for someone whose results are on the wane to find out that some financial report got them in trouble with their boss.

The attack that ensues is intended to put the financial people back in their place. The attackers accuse the finance people of being narrow-minded and overly willing to use GAAP (Generally Antagonistic Accounting Principles) to assert their narrow view of the world, while the finance people defend themselves by trumpeting GAAP as the cure for GIMP (Grossly Imprecise Management Practices).

Attempts such as these to intimidate the finance people vary in style and intensity. However the end result is almost always the same. When politics plans a field day with finance, the picnic invariably calls for

BAR-B-Q'D BEAN COUNTERS

Depending on the situation, they'll either be served up as a side dish, in a sandwich, or as the main course.

One unlucky finance guy who ended up with too much on his plate was

Side Dish Ned

Ned was the newly-appointed manager of finance for a small communications company. For years, Ned's company had followed the very time-consuming practice of preparing two separate budgets for each of the company's operating units. One budget (Plan A) was a very optimistic forecast that the manager of each operating unit would promise to the executive in charge of their region. The other budget (Plan B) was prepared by the executives in charge of each region. Their plan contained a less optimistic forecast for those same operating units. These less aggressive forecasts were then consolidated and presented to the president of the company for approval.

The regional executives had always requested a copy of Plan A and Plan B for each of their units. However, the managers in the operating units were not supposed to know anything about Plan B. If they were to learn about it, they would know that something less was expected of them.

Every year, the unit managers would let on like they knew nothing about Plan B. Yet without fail they would manage to get their hands on a copy of it. The executives never did know which budget was being managed against.

In order to remedy this situation, Ned eagerly suggested during a staff meeting that the company discontinue publishing a separate Plan B for each operating unit. He recommended that only the regional total for Plan B be published. This would provide the executives with all the information they needed to submit their budget to the president. This would also prevent the unit managers from ever finding out how much "slack" was available for their operating unit.

To the casual observer, it seemed like a simple and satisfactory solution to the problem.

Immediately following Ned's proposal, the president flatly dismissed his recommendation stating that the change would do nothing to help the company and would probably confuse everybody. When Ned tried to explain further, the president glared at him and said, "Drop the subject. Case closed."

This put-down set a bad tone for all of Ned's future interactions with the executive group. Believing that Ned was fiscally challenged when it came to the president of the company, they opted to set aside most of Ned's suggestions from that point on. Ned found himself permanently sidelined by this injury.

As put off as he was in this condition, Ned actually fared a lot better than the finance guy who ended up becoming

A Sam Sandwich

All too often, the finance people find themselves sandwiched between opposing forces bent on dominating each other.

So it was with Sam. Sam was the newly appointed Controller for a medium-sized company with a number of regional branch operations. As a new and unproven member of the management team, Sam was understandably eager to make a good impression on his fellow executives.

It wasn't long before his big break arrived. The CEO called Sam into her office and asked him to put together a confidential analysis of the company's operating costs. She wanted to know which operating units were adding costs at a faster rate than they were increasing revenues. Sam was told not to share any of the information with the operations executives until she had a chance to evaluate it herself.

Sam could hardly believe his good fortune. Here he was, the new kid on the block, working directly for the CEO of the company on an issue of major importance.

What Sam didn't know was that the Chief Operating Officer (COO) and the CEO of the company had been feuding for some time over the way the operating units should be run. The COO wanted the units to have more autonomy while the CEO wanted more control over them at headquarters. The CEO had decided that she needed evidence of any problems that the COO's approach might be causing.

That's where Sam came in. While Sam thought he had been called upon to solve a major problem for the organization, he had actually been enlisted to help the CEO fight his private war with the COO.

To his credit, Sam put together a brilliant analysis that showed where costs were getting ahead of revenues. On the day he presented it to the CEO, he was a hero.

The day after the CEO used the report to bludgeon the COO, he was a gyro.

For the next two weeks, the COO did everything possible to challenge the integrity of his report. He had the operations executives badger the accounting department for more information. He accused Sam of trying to undermine his integrity and sabotage the operations of the company.

It was Sam's unique misfortune to position himself between these two fighters, whose wayward punches managed to pulverize him after only a few short rounds.

If occasional sparring matches with the finance department aren't enough of a deterrent, the politically-minded ultimately resort to a full frontal assault. When they reach that stage, they are no longer content to discredit an isolated finance person or idea. They want nothing less than to lay siege to and topple the whole enchilada, the way they did in the case of

Main Course Margaret

Margaret was the Chief Financial Officer of an organization that was preparing to replace their entire computer system. Both the computer hardware and software that automated all of the transactions with customers had become increasingly unable to keep up with the rapid growth of the business over the last couple of years.

The company president put the head of the Information Systems (IS) department in charge of the project. Margaret was assigned the responsibility for specifying all of the functionality that the new system would need to support the various financial departments that reported to her.

From the very start, Margaret began to see some serious problems with the project plan. For one thing, the IS department was not being receptive to new requests for functionality. Without actually acknowledging it, they acted as if they had already concluded what functionality the new system would have. In addition to that, Margaret and her finance department heads were not being included in communications between the IS department and the outside vendor who had been selected to program the new software. She also had some major problems with the way her people were to be used to debug the software as it was being developed. Bugs kept re-appearing from one version to the next with no apparent explanation. The resulting process of checking and re-checking meant that the project couldn't be completed properly in the time allotted.

Her efforts to resolve the situation with the head of the IS department became more futile as time passed. Before long, it was obvious to her that the project deadline would not be met and that major changes in the project plan were necessary.

As a last resort, she took her case for a new project plan to the company president. The president, who preferred not to be involved in information systems issues, did not want to take sides in the matter.

Instead he asked that an outside consultant be brought in to assess the situation. While agreeing to this in principle, the head of IS was infuriated by this apparent challenge to his leadership of the project. From that point on, the IS department went on the offensive, accusing the finance department of having a bad attitude about the project, and contributing to the delays in its progress.

Margaret didn't feel overly threatened by these accusations. She was confident in her ability to persuade the consultant and the president that her views were justified. What Margaret overlooked was a well executed flanking maneuver from the IS chief, who proceeded to corner the consultant and convince him to help IS get the project back on track. Seeing an opportunity for greater involvement, the consultant promptly contacted the software vendor to collaborate on a new plan of attack.

At the next project status meeting which included the software vendor, the consultant and the company president, both the vendor and the consultant openly accused the finance department of withholding support for the project. The delays, they said, were due to the persistent unwillingness of Margaret and her department to work with IS in resolving outstanding issues. Their combined acknowledgment of Margaret's lack of team play put her in a rather awkward position.

Despite last-minute attempts to mount a counterattack, Margaret saw her responsibilities for the project steadily diminish from then on. By underestimating the IS department's willingness to assume attack formation to keep control of the project, Margaret's credibility was sufficiently tainted to wrest what little control she had over the project out of her hands.

Margaret's case is only one example of how an entire department's position can be easily overrun by stealthy political maneuvering. This happens even more frequently in cases where a major new business initiative must receive the endorsement of finance to get final approval.

In these cases, the fortunes of one or more executives may be at stake. If the approval of a project means that someone's executive power and influence will extend even further in the organization, they will gladly take on anyone who tries to stand in its way.

However, if a project could potentially cause financial problems, the finance people tend to line up against it. To keep the project's hopes alive, the politically astute will promptly line up their own forces opposite the finance people. This is known as

BLOCKING THE BOTTOM-LINE BACKER

One such story featured the escapades of Roger. Roger was the president and major shareholder of a privately-held corporation that provided construction materials and services to property developers and building contractors. Roger was very good at his business, but he was jealous of the developers and contractors he was servicing. They seemed to him to be the real movers, shakers and big-time moneymakers in the real estate business. More than anything, he wanted the chance to own and develop his own real estate project - one with enough scale to label him as a successful real estate developer.

It wasn't long before Roger saw an opportunity to realize his dream. One of his customers had recently converted an old apartment building into a luxury condominium community. This project was so successful that other developers began to follow suit. Through his outside contacts, Roger became aware of an apartment property that seemed to fit the bill perfectly. Roger concluded that now was the time to make good on becoming a big time developer.

First he had to put together a financial plan for the project. With some solid financial projections, he'd then be able to get approval for the project from his fellow corporate officers. Then he'd be able to obtain the necessary financing.

It fell upon the shoulders of the company's CFO to produce the financial plan. Roger figured her skill with the numbers would help him launch his new real estate venture. Within a week the plan was assembled. When the CFO met with Roger to review the numbers, things began to get ugly.

The CFO told Roger that his project involved some serious risks. Apparently, the condition of the proposed site would make its refurbishment far more difficult and time-consuming than expected. Any difficulties would extend the construction schedule well beyond the time required to cost justify it. As far as the CFO was concerned, the project could not move forward.

That was, at least, until an unknown consultant-at-large unexpectedly arrived on the scene. Roger had decided to stiff-arm his way around the CFO by hiring his own independent consultant to provide a second opinion. Miraculously, this person was able to revive the project, using considerably more optimistic estimates for construction time.

Armed with this new and improved set of projections, Roger set out to obtain the requisite approvals. After a series of long meetings with his fellow corporate officers, he was finally able to persuade them to invest not only the company's funds, but their own personal funds as well. A considerable loan was obtained, the property was acquired, and renovation was begun. The project plan called for 150 apartment units to be completely renovated and sold during a fifteen month time frame.

During the process of renovating the first couple of units, some construction problems surfaced. The construction manager started complaining that the apartment units were so old and deteriorated that they could not be renovated fast enough to stay within the project timeline and budget. When news of this unexpected development reached Roger, he replaced the construction manager and assured his colleagues that the project would proceed according to plan. His colleagues were understandably concerned, so they turned to the company's CFO to gain some more assurance.

To their total dismay, the CFO acknowledged that she had had some very serious reservations about the project from the very beginning. At their request, she prepared a memo and forwarded it to Roger for follow-up action. Instead of acting on it, he openly chastised her for acting independently without his prior approval. He then informed her that her future involvement in the project would no longer be necessary. All future project status reports would be compiled by the consultant hired by Roger - someone who could be relied upon to prepare them with the "look and feel" that he was comfortable with.

As the project continued to fall further and further behind schedule, the reports from the consultant kept claiming that the problems were only temporary. Roger's colleagues were led to believe that a breakthrough was only moments away.

By the time the project reached the end of its fifteen month schedule, fewer than 30% of the units had been fully renovated and only seventeen had been sold. The property was eventually foreclosed. The CFO, who had been precluded from investigating and reporting on its status, ended up fielding a large share of the blame for the fiasco. She subsequently resigned.

In retrospect, it would have been a lot easier on everyone if Roger had simply told the CFO from the very beginning to never challenge his opinion. An appropriate method for doing so would have been to don a sandwich board sign with big bold letters warning everyone to...

LEGGO MY EGO !!

Corporate politicians of a pack mentality always make sure that their road to success is never cluttered with contrarians. While they might enjoy the occasional run-in, they always rely on the power of intimidation to avert an actual head-on collision. To take on one of these people, you must either have a million bucks or an unending supply of steady job offers to fall back on. Since very few people fit that profile, the politicians have the odds-on advantage from the very outset. By allowing their subordinates to believe that their job is always at stake, all it takes is a potential overt threat or subtle hint of termination (p.o.t./s.h.o.t.) to drop a renegade in their tracks.

Politicians also ensure their advantage by never allowing anyone to have all of the tools they need to function independently. After all, if someone had everything they needed to perform solo, the politician wouldn't be able to influence or control the outcomes.

Placing the best qualified person in a job isn't always their goal either. People who are not independent thinkers and doers typically require the sort of perpetual care and feeding that politically astute caretakers are more than happy to dispense.

That's what Douglas learned when it came time for him to appoint a new Controller.

Douglas was the Vice President of Finance for a large oil and gas drilling company. He had been newly appointed to the position following the retirement of his predecessor. The Controller position that he previously held needed to be filled immediately. One of his first steps as a new V.P. was to begin a search for that position.

Douglas knew that his new responsibilities would prevent him from overseeing the day-to-day activities of the Controller. Therefore, he wanted to hire somebody with enough ability to take care of the difficult issues that he faced when he was Controller. His greatest concern was the quality of reporting to the headquarters. He needed someone who could handle the very demanding people who worked there. He needed someone he could depend on to provide straightforward, unbiased information that would pass muster under their considerable scrutiny.

Unbeknownst to Douglas, the CEO of the company had other ideas. The CEO was a relative newcomer himself, having recently moved over from a competitor. His particular style of management was to control everything that was said about the company's performance by reviewing and editing all information that went to headquarters. Although he was generally satisfied with Douglas' work, he found himself frequently struggling with him over the content of the HQ reports.

With the vacancy in the Controller position, the CEO saw an opportunity to strengthen his hold on the company. He already had in mind a former cohort at his previous employer. Although not the strongest candidate for the position, he knew the person could be relied upon to see things the way he did.

When Douglas presented his own list of Controller candidates to the CEO, he found himself on the receiving end of a very short and sweet ultimatum..

"As far as I'm concerned, this search is over. I've already made up my mind on this subject. No matter what you say or do, you are not going to win this one."

Having correctly interpreted this as a non-negotiable position, Douglas proceeded to hire the CEO's choice for Controller. Unable to follow through on his own convictions in the matter, Douglas suddenly found himself standing directly in the path of

THE SELF ESTEEM ROLLER

During the next year, Douglas watched as the new Controller accommodated each and every request from the CEO for changes to the HQ financial reports. Pinned between the two of them, Douglas was forced to acquiesce more and more frequently.

In less than a year, the HQ staff had became so aggravated by the constant diminution of content in the reports that they eventually insisted that the CEO "fix" the situation. While the CEO knew that he was the one responsible for this point of contention with HQ, he also knew that he could ill-afford to accept any responsibility for it. So he went along quietly, figuring the problem would eventually go away without anyone being the wiser.

But the wrath of HQ meant that a sacrifice would be necessary. The CEO and his Controller needed to quickly wash their hands of the whole matter. There, grasped firmly between them like a dirty hand towel, was Douglas. However, because the CEO did feel some guilt about the matter, he decided not to "can" his dirtied Douglas. Instead he did what he thought was the next best thing.

He hung him out to dry.

He assigned Douglas a non-financial title and hired a CFO from outside the company. Not just anyone mind you. It was someone from HQ who had once reported to Douglas, and who had been transferred to HQ due to "irreconcilable differences." The CEO saw the situation as a perfect opportunity to appease the angry gods at HQ. He would acquire someone who already had knowledge of both his business and the business at HQ. The only downside was that Douglas would report to someone he didn't get along with. The situation might prove uncomfortable for him, but it was clearly a winner for everyone else.

In the end, the gold medal went to the CEO for his politically astute engineering of the whole affair.

The silver went to the new CFO for his ability to wipe the tarnish off his tainted career.

The bronze went to the Controller who adroitly survived the entire shakeup unscathed.

Douglas, fresh from being plucked from his prized position, was left to chew on

CHICKEN OF THE "C"

The C in this case stands for Chief. It refers to the CEO, CFO, CIO or any other big chief in an organization. These are the executives who are charged with upholding the interests of everyone who has a stake in the organization, including its customers, suppliers, employees and shareholders. Occasionally, their duty to uphold those corporate interests can conflict with their own personal ones, the "chief" one being the desire to get further ahead in the organization. If upholding the company's interests means aggravating someone with the power to promote them, they will choose the path of least resistance.

Why is it that people in the upper echelons of organizations "chicken out" with such alarming regularity?

Every executive has an agenda. More often than not, those agendas include attaining higher office before their rivals do. In order to accomplish that, they make it a point not to do anything to annoy the higher-ups in the organization. At the same time, they must convince them that they are the obvious choice for advancement. The way they go about accomplishing those two goals is to use subordinates like Douglas to act as their front men and shield them from any adverse consequences from their actions (or lack thereof). The only people these leaders want in their entourage are those thick enough to stop a bullet intended for them.

Why is it that people in the lower echelons of organizations "stand up" for these executives with such alarming regularity?

They do so out of deference - deference to the leader's self-proclaimed knowledge and expertise. Positional expertise is often used by pack leaders to coerce subordinates into acknowledging the absolute power they have over everything within their span of control.

You can pretty much tell when someone is acting on self-conferred expertise. People with real expertise use their knowledge like a precision instrument to complete a mission. Those without real expertise use knowledge like a blunt instrument to beat opponents into complete submission.

Unfortunately, most people can't or won't recognize the difference when deciding if a person's leadership is truly authentic. More often than not, they accept and emulate a leader by virtue of their title and position alone. Under the right circumstances, when it serves the public interests of the business, this acclaim takes the form of hero worship. Under the wrong circumstances, when it serves the leader's private interests, it is more akin to

ZERO WORSHIP

Political leaders rely very heavily on blanket acceptance of their expertise to smother their opposition and maintain a firm hold on their status. Usually, this "expertise" stems from one major success in a specific area. When this expert knowledge catapults them into a position of power over others, their new responsibilities very often overshadow that knowledge. Rather than admit any limitations, these newfound experts resort to intimidation to overcome any challenge to their ability or authority. By never allowing opposing views to be seriously considered, and possibly validated, the political leader is able to remain on the inside track. Even when repeatedly confronted with questionable performance, these leaders continually insist on using the same tried (the word "tired" slightly transposed) and true (the word "rut" badly misspelled) formulas that they themselves originated. The prospect of another idea unseating theirs as the new way of thinking is a very real threat. Left to them, we would still be watching silent movies on black and white televisions.

That is why really good ideas rarely make it past the boardroom door. Politicians have a very subtle way of killing off ideas that they consider undesirable. By undermining the person who introduces a new idea, they manage to undermine the idea.

The tactic really works as Benjamin can attest.

Benjamin was the business analyst for a large insurance company. In the face of a noticeable increase in the customer churn rate, Benjamin took it upon himself to analyze the situation with some of the company's newer customers. His investigation uncovered some important new information about the profitability of new customers. The analysis revealed that the profile of the newer customers was considerably less in terms of purchasing power. Their rate of renewal and retention was much lower than the rate for customers who had been acquired earlier. Benjamin believed his findings made a strong case for a fundamental change in the company's strategy. His findings suggested a radical re-positioning of the company towards a more upscale type of customer.

Instead of being seriously considered, Benjamin and his ideas were severely criticized by the company's CEO.

The CEO had for quite some time realized that his longevity in the organization depended heavily upon his ability to convince his superiors that his constant focus on acquisitions was getting the desired result, namely growth. He knew that the company was purchasing more downscale customers than upscale customers in each acquisition. To limit acquisitions to the more profitable upscale customers would result in a much slower growth rate than he desired. Despite pressure from the Board of Directors about the negative impact that his acquisition strategy was having on the bottom-line, he had committed himself to this path and was not prepared to deviate from it for any reason.

When Benjamin's idea threatened to block this path, it had to be quickly pushed aside. The revelation about the declining profitability of newly acquired customers was promptly dismissed as frivolous.

After all, the company had been operating the same way for years with these "less profitable" customers and there was nothing to indicate that it couldn't continue to do so successfully. The CEO asserted that Benjamin was way out of line because the company could easily find ways to make these customers more profitable. His criticism of Benjamin effectively sidestepped the whole issue of customer purchasing power.

But it did not manage to resolve it.

Three years later, the company was eventually forced to scale back its acquisitions after suffering a series of major setbacks in its profit margins. The CEO's course of action, while politically expedient, was inconsistent with sound business principles.

This left the company's remaining executives, who had no clue how to deal with the situation, to ponder why nothing new ever seemed to happen, and to lament...

"I can't believe it's not better!"

Before concluding this part of the story, it must be said that those who use aggressive and occasionally subversive tactics to prevail do not limit their attentions to only those with contrarian points of view. They can be particularly condescending towards those less willing or able to fight back. These attitudes can cause them to construe members of the opposite sex, race or religion as being members of the opposing sex, race or religion. Preferring to keep their competition to a minimum, they tend to endorse the concept that in management, opposites detract. In a world where everything is supposed to revolve around them, these people are known as

THE GLASS CEILING FANS

They are easily recognizable by their trademark. Their trademark is contempt...contempt for anyone less willing to use brute force to get ahead in the organization. While no business leader in their right mind would openly endorse that sort of attitude, its existence is still evident in many boardrooms. When those who become leaders appear unable to act like leaders, it is probably because the task of becoming a leader was less equal for some than it was for others.

CHAPTER SUMMARY

Corporate politicians with a pack mentality are, by nature, dedicated to the proposition that all (wo)men are intimidated equal.

While the tactics they employ to remain atop the pecking order may differ in intensity, the intent is always the same. Their sole purpose is to serve notice to anyone thinking about challenging them that they'll have a fight on their hands if they try. Intimidators know that most organization people have been tamed by their belief in mutual cooperation, having been taught to use facts, not force, to advance their position. They take full advantage of this civilized behavior by forcing a confrontation on every issue. They count on the fact that most people will choose to avoid conflict altogether or back down once a fight starts to escalate.

This extraordinary ability to quell any sort of challenge to their own authority is used on a variety of fronts. To protect their most vulnerable areas, they often resort to a *side-show of force* to keep potential challengers off balance. By making a federal case out of a minor incident, they manage to fix people's gaze on the trivial instead of the crucial aspects of the business. Their show of strength on insignificant issues also serves to divert attention away from major weaknesses in their own areas of responsibility.

The ever-present threat of a full frontal assault is usually more than enough to keep most would-be challengers at bay. However, there are always those occasional flareups that occur when someone acting on behalf of the organization is unable to resist the urge to test the limits of their leaders. In every pack there are those who occasionally "tug the leash" to see if it's still holding them back. They typically learn quickly that pack leaders always keep a firm grip on it. The yank they receive at the end of *the feud chain* convinces most would-be challengers not to try it again.

Understanding the motivations of intimidators is all about understanding their limits and boundaries. In their case, one has to be both a mind reader and a map reader to safely traverse the corporate landscape. These people don't believe in boundaryless organizations. Guided by the *Usurp, U pay* principle, the penalty they mete out to those who stray onto their turf is quite severe. Intimidators use the threat of retaliation to shield their own weaknesses from the rest of the organization. If an organization's performance does start to decline, an intimidator's worst nightmare is to have someone attribute it to someone or something under their span of control.

If performance continues to decline, the pack mentality becomes more pronounced. Instead of closing ranks, pack leaders start closing borders. Instead of exploring hands-on solutions to problems, they enforce hands-off policies to keep outsiders away. The resulting lack of failure analysis makes it possible for them to perpetuate inept behavior without the fear of discovery. *Truth decay* eventually sets in as the perpetrators rationalize their behavior and downplay the significance of the organization's problems. The most effective intimidators do more than simply rationalize inappropriate behavior. They legitimize it. By underscoring the insignificant and undermining the opposition, they manage to thwart any bona fide attempts to get at the truth. Anyone inclined to challenge their systematic *facts evasion* is met with contempt and openly criticized for being negative and unsupportive of the organization and its goals.

Those in the organization charged with the responsibility for identifying and resolving problems become polarized by this mindset. Accountants, auditors and finance people in particular find themselves on the defensive as their legitimate attempts to uncover weaknesses provoke hostile responses from the leadership. Repeated shell shock eventually leads to acquiescence. Instead of being allowed to function as legitimate business partners, the finance people are forced to do *the math of least resistance* so they won't be subjected to *accost accounting* and end up as *bar-b-q'd bean counters*.

Despite these concessions, the finance people, by virtue of their role as guardians of the corporate treasure trove, cannot always avoid confrontation with those seeking to expand their empire with help from the company checkbook. Whenever some new venture promises to advance the interests of the few or the one, the amount of objectivity afforded the finance people diminishes as the amount of money involved increases. At the first sign of resistance, the proponents of the project promptly use intimidation tactics to damage the credibility of the number crunchers and sway the opinion of the decisionmakers. By ganging up on the finance people, and impugning their integrity, the pack mentality succeeds in *blocking the bottom line backer* from pursuing other, potentially more profitable projects.

In the realm of politics, it was once the primary purpose of government to preserve or extend the reach of its empire. In the realm of business, corporate politicians now carry that torch by making it their primary goal to preserve and expand their corporate empires.

Politicians of the pack persuasion are incredibly ego driven when it comes to this particular goal. In their case, ego might just as well stand for **E**mpire **G**rabbing **O**pportunist. These egos have little or no tolerance for contrarian points of view. Armed with colloquialisms such as "More is Better", "Stop or Grow" and "Volume is King", these militants campaign relentlessly for more territory, no matter what the cost. The prospect of losing momentum to shore up weaknesses is anathema to them. Those brave enough to go head-to-head with them and demand accountability can expect to hear *"leggo my ego"* ringing in their ears as they wonder what ran them over. Finding their future career path suddenly flattened, they come to realize that it was the *self esteem roller* that leveled them.

This all seems strange to those whose modern day business thinking suggests that good ideas should be allowed to stand on their own merits. Nonetheless, the politically motivated will choose to advance only those ideas that they themselves originated. Afraid of the possible ramifications of someone else's idea, a *Chicken of the "C"* wants to make sure everyone strictly adheres to their way of thinking.

And they usually succeed. In the world of business, there is absolutely no shortage of obsessive obedience to leaders of questionable caliber. Those most responsible for this excess are typically neophytes and underachievers who depend on whatever goodwill these leaders have to offer. When the object of their adoration is an executive whose business acumen is strong in one area and seriously limited in others, most are unable or unwilling to discern the difference. They proceed to accept everything these leaders say and do on faith. Their blanket acceptance constitutes a form of *zero worship* that ultimately suppresses the kind of original thinking that every organization needs to prosper.

The resulting absence of any meaningful new ideas can prove deadly to even the healthiest of organizations. If intimidation causes idea-making to become the exclusive domain of the company's leadership, the people in the organization who are closest to the customer become alienated. As their input dwindles, the voice of the customer grows fainter and fainter. When the customer is no longer being heard at the highest levels of the organization, things eventually start to deteriorate. The deterioration sets off a barrage of generally imprecise thinking on the part of management. When the actions they take produce nothing in the way of improvement, they begin to turn on themselves.

But not until after they've turned on their subordinates. With unbridled contempt for people's feelings and sensitivities, they assail those who are, by virtue of their personal or professional status, less inclined to fight back. Convinced that their shortcomings stemmed from someone else's lack of resolve, they let their intolerance for failure evolve into an intolerance for anyone less aggressive than they are. Armed with this self-inflicted superiority complex, these *glass ceiling fans* end up punishing the organization by closing both their minds and their doors to those with a real penchant for the business and a genuine passion for the customer.

Yet despite all of their brute force, pack leaders do eventually lose control of the situation. In attempting to undermine their critics, they undermine the ability of the organization to sustain itself. By silencing criticism, they also stifle the critical thinking that is essential for improving performance. In an intimidating environment, people who start shrinking become people who stop thinking. When the pool of knowledge about customers, suppliers and competitors eventually dries up, all that remains in a once-competitive company are inconsequential opinions and anecdotes for the leaders to argue about.

CHAPTER 4

CONSPIRING IN THE COLONY

Colonies live by an unruly code of conduct. Led by their queens, they try to expand their empire by regularly invading other colonies. They raid the other colonies, steal the offspring and put them to work in their own colony. One particular species of ant has members whose heads are so big that it is beneath them to do anything for themselves. Instead they rely totally on the worker ants to feed them everything they need to survive.

Another species of ant has a tendency to initiate hostile takeovers on a regular basis. Here, a young queen will hang around with another species of ant until she is finally accepted by their workers. Once taken inside by these workers, she then scopes out the competition, eventually going so far as to ride the back of the reigning queen. When the time is right, she beheads the reigning queen and takes over the entire colony.

In termite colonies, life revolves around the king and queen. The workers must constantly build and repair the nest. They must also be ready to take care of things in case the pair "lays an egg." The soldiers of the species are expected to sacrifice everything for the safety and preservation of the colony.

With all those soldiers working single-mindedly to preserve their leader's legacy, it's no wonder why mounds of them manage to endure for countless numbers of years.

In the corporate world, you're part of a colony if you're faced with some decidedly opportunistic leaders surrounded by a bunch of acquiescent followers.

The colonial organization is less tyrannical than the pack, but it has a few of its own less- than-desirable qualities.

Among them are:

Leaders who are self-centered and not self-reliant.
Leaders whose primary focus is empire-building.
Followers who excessively cater to the needs of their leaders.
Followers who are overly obliging and not very discriminating.

In this type of environment, the leaders have somehow managed to convince their followers that they are deserving of their full trust and respect. More often than not, the leaders in this situation may be fairly new to the organization, having recently joined it via a merger or acquisition, or having been recruited from the outside.

Whatever the reason, they enter their new environment as a complete unknown. Their cohorts, who want to believe in the ability and integrity of their new leader, tend not to question their motives at the outset. This honeymoon period lasts as long as the leadership continues to persuade them that they hold the keys to future prosperity.

As both sides outwardly embrace each other in their mutual quest for success, each side harbors a different view of what that success should look like.

To the followers, who believe their longevity with the organization depends upon how well they perform, the end game is getting results in the form of greater revenues and profits.

To the leaders, the end game is longevity ... period. They believe that by staying in the game long enough and outlasting the inevitable ups and downs in performance, the big payoff will be waiting for them at the end of the line.

If longevity is the secret to their success, what is the secret to their longevity?

The answer lies in their ability to convince everyone around them that they are remarkably gifted. Without actually being forced to substantiate their views and opinions, they are permitted to grab center stage and run the show. What the people who hired them don't realize is the fact that these views and opinions tend to be highly personal and non-negotiable in nature. When push comes to shove, they're going to find out that the clairvoyant they thought they hired is in fact

THE TUNNEL VISION-ARY

In political circles, longevity doesn't depend upon what you lead people to do. It depends on what you lead them *to believe*. After a while, followers start to believe more of what their leaders are saying, and less in what they themselves are actually doing for the organization. Left unchecked, this kind of behavior will result in a company that depends on a belief system rather than a business system for its identity. Eventually, it will find itself relying more on anecdotes than actions to accomplish its purpose.

Politically-minded leaders are the most adept at transforming (twisting?) a business system into a belief system. By doing so, they put themselves in position to impose their own set of beliefs on others. In most cases, these beliefs assert that there is one and only one right way to look at the business. Contrarian viewpoints are occasionally entertained, but almost always dismissed.

Because it takes time for the leader's belief system to take hold, something has to take place in the interim to make sure that opposing views can't derail the new leader's agenda. The leaders know that the worst thing they can do is provide potential challengers with idle time to concoct their own initiatives. In order to keep the opposition busy and keep the illusion of progress alive, these leaders engage their organizations in various business-like activities. These activities are cleverly designed to maintain the image of a company that is trying to solve problems.

In reality, the company is not trying to solve problems. It is trying to solve an equation.

In its commercial form, the equation looks like this...

BUSINESS = ACTION.

However, when this equation is contorted into its political form, it becomes...

BUSYNESS = ACTIVITY.

These two equations, which look so much alike, have one simple and major difference.

The first equates to a high level of performance. The second does not.

The first equation is based on a very sound business principle. It states that for a business to be successful, it must take action to capitalize on its strengths and opportunities, while addressing any weaknesses and threats. Before actions are taken, the business should determine in advance what sort of strategy it intends to follow. Once the desired outcomes are clearly determined and articulated, the business can structure its approach accordingly. That ensures that the actions taken produce the results desired.

The second equation is based on a very political principle. It states that for a leader to achieve longevity in his or her position, there must be a continuous level of activity aimed at resolving a perceived fault in the system. Before these activities are actually undertaken, it should be determined in advance if the outcome of these activities will reinforce positions that the leader has already taken on the issues. That ensures that the leader's position will always be authenticated.

When an organization gets caught up in that sort of self-serving activity, it starts to matter less and less whether any meaningful results are achieved or anything new is accomplished. In these types of situations, those who follow the leader are more concerned about being supportive than they are about the quality of the outcomes. Leaders can put forth anecdotal hypotheses, often based on flawed assumptions, and consume vast amounts of their people's time doing analysis that usually leads nowhere.

If you're a manager in an organization that operates this way, each time you're called upon to investigate some problem you're probably being sent on

A BUSYNESS TRIP

Being sent on a busyness trip means doing work that is an end in itself, not the means to an end.

It means that someone else will lead the way and you've been chosen to tote the baggage on a journey that leads to nowhere.

As the business manager for a large manufacturer of machine parts, Donna knew the difference between business and busyness. She had a reputation for always finding her way to the bottom line. Her no-nonsense approach was often astonishing to those whose operations she would periodically analyze.

That was until the day the company hired a new head of manufacturing.

From day one, Donna could see that the new guy had a special agenda. It was the sort of agenda that you wouldn't find published in the hiring announcement. From what she could tell, it seemed as though the new chief was almost immediately ill-contented with his scope of authority. She sensed that he was going to make a case very early on to take over some more areas of responsibility that were currently beyond his jurisdiction.

Within thirty days of his being hired, Donna's suspicions were confirmed.

Donna had recalled from her very first meeting with him that he had requested information about areas of the company that were in need of some shoring up. Presumably, this information was needed to help him "manage up" those areas for which he had responsibility and to "manage around" those areas outside his control. Donna suspected he was trying to get something on the people whose areas were outside his control. She advised him that the area most in need of major improvement was an area in materials management that he controlled. She reviewed the history of problems that the area had, and she offered some possible solutions based on discussions she had already had with some of its personnel.

The new chief took this information very gladly. He thanked Donna profusely for her insight into this major opportunity for improvement in his operations. He genuinely seemed as though he was ready to start dealing with some of the problems in his own backyard.

And then something interesting happened. The staff who worked in Donna's department began to inform her that they were receiving a lot of time-consuming requests for information from the manufacturing group about the performance of the shipping department. Donna considered this strange for two reasons. First, none of the requests had been directed through her, as was normally the case. Second, the shipping function was outside the scope of the new manufacturing chief's responsibilities. Why weren't the requests for information being channeled through the head of the shipping department?

The answer soon became obvious.

Based on allegations made by the materials manager who reported to him, the new chief had concluded that the problems attributed to manufacturing were due to problems in shipping. The materials manager who made the allegations happened to be responsible for the area that Donna had recommended for change. In order to save face with his new boss, the manager had improperly asserted that problems with the product were due to improper packaging and shipping, not bad materials. By choosing to believe these assertions without demanding proof, the chief of operations saw his opportunity to take control of shipping. The requests for information, which were requiring so much time from Donna's resources, were an attempt to substantiate those spurious allegations against the shipping department.

This tactic, albeit underhanded, worked perfectly. Within six months, the responsibility for shipping was reassigned to the head of manufacturing.

Even though it was revealed shortly thereafter that materials management was in fact responsible for the problems instead of shipping, it was too late to remedy the situation.

Was this an extreme case of corporate politics or simply business as usual?

It isn't business as usual when major decisions are made based on deliberate misconceptions. For the politicians who perpetrate these myths, it's more like...

BUSINESS AS USE-U-ALL

Politically-minded operatives have a hard time limiting themselves to overthrowing only one or two departments. When two leaders in an organization end up squaring off against each other in a winner-take-all contest, the ensuing confrontation can embroil nearly everyone in the organization. All it takes is for each side to have equal access to the resources of the company. Given that, they will engage those resources in every way possible to undermine each other.

Don will be the first to tell you how true this is. Don was the head of Information Systems in a company where the Chief Financial Officer (CFO) and the Chief Operating Officer (COO) decided to take each other on in a hostile bid for the CEO spot which was about to be vacated by the incumbent. The CFO had concluded that the COO posed the greatest threat to his succession plans. He was ready to poke a few holes in the COO's performance to prevent him from making further headway towards the corner office.

It wasn't long before Don and his counterparts in Human Resources and Finance were all being asked by each side to compile information against the other. The CFO had the Finance people trying to show how the COO's policies in certain areas were hurting revenues and profits. The COO had the Information Systems department report how the CFO's financial procedures were causing recurring system problems. Human Resources was helping the COO make a case against the salary guidelines imposed by the CFO while, at the same time, helping the CFO demonstrate why the high level of turnover was responsible for staffing problems in the COO's areas.

Whether or not any of the analysis does anything to improve the organization's performance is of little consequence during these types of power struggles. The troops in the trenches scurry around frantically trying to be responsive while doing everything they can to avoid the line of fire.

In the midst of all this distraction, the line managers who try to go about their business of managing the work force are in reality

MANAGING THE WORK FARCE

In organizations that operate like termite colonies, the workers focus almost exclusively on helping their leaders expand their empire. They shield their leader from any real day-to-day responsibility, and do damage control if and when the leader makes a mistake.

Amidst all of this leader-focused behavior, the business itself receives only a fraction of the attention it needs to operate properly. Followers who become fixated on their leaders become increasingly insensitive to the needs of their co-workers and customers. Concerns about how well the organization is performing give way to concerns about how well a particular leader is doing. Followers are no longer convinced that their opportunities for advancement are tied to results. Instead they believe their success is tied to their leader's coattails. Business decisions are based less upon the particular merits of the proposals involved and more upon the upward mobility of the people involved.

Politically-minded leaders who become the beneficiaries of all this attention and adulation are the most adept at exploiting it to the fullest extent possible. For anyone willing to subjugate their own interests in exchange for leader-favored status, these leaders will promptly lay down the

WELCOME DOOR MAT

In situations where employees choose to serve the special interests of a particular leader to the exclusion of the legitimate interests of their organization, there is an unavoidable aspect of human nature at work. In virtually every person who serves in an organization there is a common and very highly developed instinct. That instinct is to find success by following a successful leader.

Beginning with our parents and teachers, we are brought up to believe that our value as human beings is based on our ability to take direction from those in authority. We are educated at an early age to subordinate our own thinking to theirs. Later, as adults in a business setting, there is very little that we feel free to do in an organization without first getting permission from someone in authority.

As a result of this upbringing, the majority of business people believe their leader should be the starting point (the alpha) for everything they set out to accomplish. Astute business people know how to capitalize on this willingness to follow by pointing their people in a direction that proves to be of value to the organization (the omega).

Things start heading in the wrong direction when leaders somehow manage to take advantage of people's instinctive desire to be good followers by making themselves both the alpha and the omega for everything that gets accomplished. Even though it is unrealistic and unconscionable for a leader to expect everyone's actions to accrue to their own personal benefit, that doesn't stop the politically astute from doing everything possible to see it happen.

Leaders who are masters at corporate politics are particularly adept at taking advantage of followers who, for whatever reason, are less capable of thinking and acting independently in ways that benefit the organization. Often these are people in middle management whose lack of understanding of the business leaves them vulnerable to the politician's power of suggestion.

Rather than prune these people from the ranks of management, political leaders use their inability to their own advantage. Instead of following a legitimate business agenda, they are given the leader's personal agenda to work on. Because it takes a considerable amount of continuous effort to find, recruit and develop this kind of following, you can always expect to find the politicos...

WORKING ON THE WEAKENED

By convincing their quarry that it is okay to trade away competence and credibility in exchange for loyalty, the politicos manage to amass a following that is often the envy of their peers.

To convince their special followers that their loyalty will take them places in the organization that their absence of talent can not, the leaders entice them with gifts.

These gifts induce the prospective followers into pledging undying allegiance in return for protection from any outside forces that might threaten their already tenuous position in the organization. These inducements are known as

DUTY-FREE GIFTS

Duty-free gifts are not the tangible kind, of course. They're more like unspoken promises, exchanged on a quid-pro-quo basis. They provide a mutual guarantee that both the leader and the follower will somehow see things the same way if their conduct in a given situation is ever questioned. In exchange for this mutual guarantee of support, the leader bestows upon the follower something akin to an easement.

An easement is a free pass, an automatic variance. It's a sort of unwritten insurance policy that protects its beneficiary against slip-ups suffered in the line of duty. These types of easements are an absolutely essential part of the bargain between leader and follower. Because the follower steadfastly agrees to advance the leader's agenda in all business dealings, there are inevitably those situations where the follower's conduct might be challenged by others in the organization. The easement guarantees that the person most able to shield the follower from the consequences, i.e. the leader, will intervene and help rationalize the questionable behavior, making it possible for the follower to emerge completely intact.

It's never too hard to tell when a leader and a follower have exchanged these gifts.

Take the case of Richard for example. Richard was an easement waiting to happen.

Ever since the day his boss hired him, Richard had been in and out of hot water. The only thing constant in Richard's department was turmoil. On more than one occasion, there had been situations where it was perfectly obvious to a lot of people that problems were rampant in his area of the business. Responsibilities were not being handled properly. Error rates had reached alarming levels and customer complaints had reached an all-time high. The crown jewel involved an outside consultant who was brought in to remedy the deteriorating situation.

The consultant was brought in to figure out a way to reduce the high rate of errors and customer complaints. Based on input from Richard, the consultant ended up making a lot of bad estimates about the department's activity levels, which ended up contributing to even more errors and complaints.

Somehow, Richard emerged completely unharmed by all of this.

By quickly intervening and attributing the problems in Richard's area to the consultant, Richard's boss was able to absolve him of any responsibility for the fiasco. Despite his history of problems with managing the department, these apparent shortcomings were packaged by Richard's boss as someone else's problem.

Thanks to the benefit of his easement, someone else got stuck holding the thorns so Richard could end up smelling like a rose.

There are some cases in which followers will not even require the gift of an easement before swearing undying loyalty to their leader. In these instances, the followers are automatically convinced that the leader already has their best interests at heart and will do what is best for them at every opportunity. Some attribute this to an over-reliance on divine intervention, probably because it conjures up images of a

NAIVETÉ SCENE

Followers in this situation don't perceive the need for protection from those outside their leader's domain. They may be more self-confident in their own abilities and more determined to achieve favored status without special treatment.

These people make it particularly easy for politically astute leaders to advance their agenda in the organization. Without having to stop to forge secret alliances with everyone in the trenches, these leaders can take for granted the unconditional support of those who view both themselves and their leader as infallible.

When followers mesmerize themselves this way, they also suffer from tunnel vision. The focus of their behavior becomes very narrow. Their judgment becomes impaired by concerns over who will be the ultimate beneficiary of certain information that is obtained, or certain actions that are taken. If they are convinced that their leader will be harmed by something, they will purposefully stand in its way and try to prevent it from happening. Like termites protecting their queen, they will go to any lengths necessary to prevent any misfortune from befalling their leader.

Executives with good political instincts never cease to capitalize on this loyalty by initiating conflict when it serves their purpose. That's not to say that conflict is bad. It just needs to be timed properly for it to work properly. Good business leaders typically encourage conflict when ideas are in the planning stages. Formal debates take place to flesh out all of their strengths and weaknesses. When all arguments, both pro and con, have been heard, a decision is made and both sides close ranks behind that decision.

In corporate politics, decision makers aren't constrained by such orderly rules of conduct.

This is especially true in cases where politically motivated executives find themselves in crisis situations where they are called upon to make drastic changes in their organization. Drastic change is never a politician's best friend, so many will reach for some sort of stopgap measure to slow things down a bit. In other words, if a corporate politician is opposed to a change of pace, (s)he will try to control the pace of change. The more pressure there is for change, the more resourceful they become. Politically savvy executives simply resort to tried and true techniques for bringing even the most rambunctious change agents to their knees. It's their way of...

WINNING BY WEARING DOWN

The two most effective tactics involve the use of a divide and conquer strategy. The smart politician knows that most people cannot resist the urge to put in their two cents on any subject. They conveniently use that element of human nature to their own advantage. When they need to delay, disrupt or sidetrack an impending decision, the politicos know that every organization has a wellspring of upwardly mobile, career-minded individuals who are constantly seeking greater involvement in high-level decisions. All they need do to stymie the decision is to invite these eager beavers into the process and solicit opinions from them in one of two ways.

The first approach is a clever ploy whereby a leader will engage two or more people to work on the exact same assignment at the same time, without informing them about the others' involvement. Employee A goes off thinking (s)he has full responsibility for the outcome of the project, not knowing that somewhere else in the organization, B and C are thinking the exact same thing about themselves. Each is told to report their progress directly to the leader. The leader manages to keep them all moving along separate paths, working towards different conclusions. Once assured of different outcomes, the leader then assembles everyone in the same room and goads them into defending their conclusions. As each one tries desperately to advance their position, the leader pits them against each other.

The second technique comes into play when leaders sense that progress is being made towards a consensus that they aren't comfortable with. In order to head it off, they simply invite more participants in at the tail end of the process. By soliciting multiple rounds of last-minute input from the ranks of understandably eager, and equally uninformed wanna-bees, the leader can generate enough controversy to park any decision in a permanent holding pattern.

Politicians who are particularly adept at using these techniques can actually force a recently completed decision process to begin all over again. To the untrained eye, it appears that the leader is acting responsibly by making absolutely sure that the best decision is made. It all appears perfectly innocent because the technique is applied without any undue pressure being exerted on anyone. Every invitation that is sent out requesting another opinion from somebody else is done with the utmost politeness.

(Did you know the word politics is actually an extension of the word "polite?")

This technique makes it possible for the politician to question everything and accomplish nothing by engaging in a form of subterfuge. Meanwhile, those responsible for reaching a decision become increasingly frustrated as they attempt to reconcile an unending horde of conflicting opinions. Waiting to pull the trigger or the plug on the decision, they keep being told over and over...

"Ready..Aim...........Ready..."

Sometimes, the process becomes so frustrating and fatiguing that no final decision is ever reached. The result is a lot of hard feelings between the parties who recommended the decision and those who were recruited to help defeat it. For the vanquished, the urge to retaliate becomes almost irrepressible. When that happens, and you happen to be one of the people who volunteered those unwanted opinions, you'll probably be in line to receive

A PENANCE FOR YOUR THOUGHTS

It's never the politician they retaliate against. They go directly to the source of those derelict opinions. Those unfortunate enough to be on the receiving end find they have nowhere to hide and no one to protect them. Meanwhile, the corporate politician who solicited all the controversy emerges with his secret agenda completely intact. Having successfully undermined the decision process, (s)he is free to continue cruising down the road they've paved with the status quo.

As the status quo continually prevails, the organization stops trying to change any of its priorities or management responsibilities. Even when the behavior of customers or competitors starts to change, an organization that is working the status quo will often fail to shift its own set of priorities to maintain a competitive advantage.

History has taught that for an organization to truly succeed and thrive, it has to be very dynamic. If the push for change slowly or suddenly stops, an overwhelming sense of complacency can set in. Unless someone or something quickly displaces this sense of contentment with the status quo, things start to stagnate. A stagnant environment, like stagnant water, can breed undesirable elements. Corporate politics thrives in this sort of environment. It takes root during extended periods of inertia when leaders choose to rest on their laurels and fail to challenge the status quo with new ideas and initiatives.

Inertia also provides the political elements with the perfect opportunity to broaden their boundaries within the organization. With a degree of zeal reminiscent of the crusades, they embark upon a quest to convert the corporate masses and expand...

THE HOLEY ROAMIN' EMPIRE

Corporate politicians have an instinctive need to expand their empires and their influence. During extended periods of leader-induced inertia, performance-oriented behavior subsides in favor of ego-centered behavior. Without being forced to focus on better ways to perform for employees, customers and stockholders, the politically-minded are free to focus on finding better ways to make the organization protect and serve their own interests.

One of the best ways of accomplishing that is to annex new territory.

However, before new territory can be acquired, existing territory must first be adequately safeguarded from the threat of invasion. You can tell when a political leader is preparing to embark on a territorial conquest when (s)he begins to exhibit

Protective-Compulsive Behavior

This kind of behavior manifests itself when the management of a particular department or function begins to noticeably deteriorate and no one in the organization bothers to question it. In actuality, the head of the department may be overwhelmed, or the situation may be out of control. While a simple change in management or a concerted effort by employees could produce a turnaround in the situation, the situation goes unchallenged and unchanged for fear that an inquiry might reveal some rather long-standing neglect in that particular area of the business. The fear stems from an unwillingness to question the issue, especially when a corporate politician could turn out to be the one responsible for it.

Those who avoid this confrontation know full well that politicians are compelled to protect their people and image from being tarnished by performance-related issues. Political leaders never allow their road to future power and prosperity to be "curbed" by these sorts of issues.

In the case of Richard, the leader promptly came to his rescue when it looked as though events had overtaken him.

Richard's boss knew that to remain in contention for a higher ranking job in the company, he would have to do more than cover up Richard's underperformance with a series of simple rationalizations. He was going to have to demonstrate that Richard had actually succeeded in exposing problems caused by others and was deserving of more responsibility. He accomplished this feat by blaming the consultant and other departments in the company for the breakdown in performance. He heralded Richard as the progressive thinker who had courageously undertaken the task of restructuring his department. He effectively distanced Richard from all of the negative consequences of his own actions. He was able to promote Richard on the basis of his willingness to accept increased responsibility, despite considerable evidence that suggested his inability to handle it.

Richard's boss didn't do any of that out of the goodness of his heart. Like every other corporate politician, he had an agenda - one that was motivated by

Acquisitive-Obsessive Behavior

When a business-oriented leader looks at a department, (s)he typically sees a specific operating function with activities and accountabilities that are distinguishable from those in other departments.

When a corporate politician looks at a department, (s)he sees a fiefdom just waiting to be annexed to their growing empire.

While it may all be "greek" to those unsuspecting targets who find themselves caught in the cross-hairs, the rules of encroachment clearly specify the politically correct manner of ambush to employ when a renegade department needs to be

DELTA COUP D'ETAT

The politicos know that in order to shift the balance of power in their favor, they must alter the equation that determines how control is distributed in the organization.

Departments controlled by corporate politicians operate according to the following simple equation:

$$Quantity > Quality$$

In their quest to expand their empire, these politicians typically run up against other departments whose business equation is quite the opposite of theirs. These are departments that eschew doing lots of volume in favor of doing everything accurately. Their equation is

$$Quality > Quantity$$

Departments such as these who "play the game by the numbers" often fail to see how inviting a target they are for those who are better at "playing the numbers game." Corporate politicians build and govern their organizational empires according to the law of large numbers. Every attempt they make to orchestrate a takeover begins with the same overture - an overture that challenges the validity of the Quantity/Quality equation in a particular area of the business. If they can convince the powers-that-be that the need for quantities of scale outweigh the need for quality of output, they can eventually overtake their target.

That was the experience of Ted, who saw his department overtaken by an onslaught of politically motivated attacks from a separate organization in the company. Ted was a perfect example of the output from another basic equation that governs the world of politically-motivated takeovers. The equation states that for every corporate politician who has traversed this road to success, there must be an equal and opposite number of people left behind as

THE ROAD-KILL TO SUCCESS

Ted was the manager responsible for recording and processing customer shipping requests for a major interstate trucking company. Ted's previous background in accounting and auditing had made him the preferred choice for this position due to the perceived need for accurate recording and transmittal of this customer information. Ted brought to the management of this function all of the discipline of an internal auditor. Customer orders had to be constantly checked and re-checked. Errors had to be promptly identified, researched and resolved.

Nearby in an adjacent facility, the logistics department was trying to develop more cost-effective shipping routes. This department had been experiencing some significant problems in recent years. Shipping costs had been steadily increasing and competitors had been taking business away. The department was headed by Robert, an individual who believed that the solution to the problems in his department was greater control over the activities in other departments. The fact that Ted's people had control over all of the order-related information and communications with customers was particularly irksome to him. He was convinced he could make greater use of Ted's function by using the information for logistics purposes.

Given his financial background, Ted was steadfast in his belief that the handling of customer account-related issues should remain independent from other functions. Despite his skill with the figures, he didn't figure his intractable position constituted an engraved invitation for a takeover attempt from his rival in logistics. Knowing that the logistics department had enough problems of its own to deal with, Ted mistakenly believed that his department would be allowed to remain independent - just the way it had been for the last ten years.

When the surprise attack came, Ted was caught flat-footed. By preceding his hostilities with a well-executed and highly influential propaganda campaign, Robert had managed to convince the company's president that his problems in logistics were close to being resolved. He asserted that he could easily absorb Ted's responsibilities with little or no disruption in either area. The two-sided proposition that he made to win control of Ted's area was a reduction in cost due to consolidation as well as an improvement in logistics. By effectively downplaying the full extent of his own department's shortcomings, Robert was able to ensure that the issue of quality never played a part in the decision.

Rumors of the impending change started flying between the two departments. Before long, it was obvious to everyone that a changing of the guard was imminent. What they didn't know was that Robert was about to be named the new

ERROR APPARENT

After Ted lost control of his areas, the logistics group began to focus less on quality control issues with customer accounts and more on scheduling issues. As the shipping order error rate started to grow, more and more customers began taking their business elsewhere.

So what happened to Robert?

He ended up moving to another area and getting promoted because his boss, the V.P. of Operations, was able to insulate him from the failures that took place in his organization. For the V.P., it was a simple matter of deflecting criticism back towards others in the executive group who had not delivered additional funds and human resources that he had requested to deal with the quality control problems. He made it look as though his fellow executives were responsible for their escalation. By cleverly managing to conceal the fact that it was his own suggestion to have Robert take over Ted's area, the V.P. ended up looking the part of the innocent victim rather than the guilty perpetrator.

This remarkable ability of political higher-ups to insulate themselves from the ill effects of their own decisions is known as

DIPLOMATIC IMMUNITY

There is a school of business thinking that requires every major organizational initiative to be thoroughly evaluated and documented in advance, and then managed throughout its duration. By clearly specifying the deliverables and the due dates, it effectively thwarts subsequent attempts to alter a project's specifications and extend the timetable for its completion. It also makes it possible to periodically evaluate progress and correct shortcomings in the management of the project.

Don't expect to find this school of thinking anywhere on the campus of corporate politics. The political code of conduct is silent on the subject of performance specifications and evaluations, especially those involving sound quantitative or other empirical measurements. Without these annoying guideposts to demarcate a lack of results, the politically motivated are free to conduct business affairs as beauty contests. Graduates of their C.H.A.R.M. (Cultivating Highly Aesthetic Relationship Managers) School know that when it comes to getting ahead, it is always better to look good than to be good. They also know that when people see someone who looks good say something that sounds good, they believe it always turns out good.

How do you know if your organization has matriculated into this school of thought?

The telltale signs are an irrepressible, steady stream of status reports that look and sound more like election day speeches than factually-based assessments of management performance.

Take for instance this very creative explanation of an actual situation.

ACTUAL SITUATION

The sales department of a company recently experienced a sudden downturn in its performance due to an unexpected decrease in its workforce. The decrease stemmed from a failure to enforce hiring policies designed to ensure the right number and the right kind of personnel on staff at all times. With the resulting shortage of people available to fill orders, the available sales staff were overworked in a desperate attempt to overcome the problem.

In response to the problem, the department manager conducted a major recruitment effort at the last minute, filling the empty positions with a number of marginally qualified people. Due to their lack of qualifications and experience, and despite an eleventh-hour attempt to train them, these recruits were essentially unable to handle any of the sales volume during the month.

RESULTING REPORT

"The sales department enjoyed another very strong month's worth of activity which pushed the productivity of the sales force to its highest level this year. The sales staff handled 68 orders per person this month compared to an average of 53 year to date.

The department responded quickly to an expected increase in demand by maintaining staffing at the planned level and significantly increasing the level and frequency of training.

Anticipated increases in the level of employee turnover were addressed by stepped-up recruiting efforts which yielded a significant number of new hires during the month. The department is now poised to produce at a record pace for the balance of the year."

EPILOGUE

Unless an organization is prepared to routinely audit its various operations, it has no real means of ferreting out these sorts of misrepresentations. When it must rely on the integrity of each manager to fully and accurately disclose the situation in their area, the politicos can milk it for all it's worth - and make themselves look magnificent in the process.

The kind of diplomatic immunity that is granted to politicos in high places gets magnified when they have the opportunity to divert attention away from shortcomings in their own organization by setting their sights on another organization.

That's why you will always find them

LOOKING FOR MR. GOOD BARGAIN

Statistics show that in cases where one company acquires another, two out of three fail to achieve their financial objectives.

When these failures are reported in the financial press, the reasons most often stated are a failure to achieve synergies or a clash in corporate cultures and management styles.

What the financial press doesn't dwell on are the acquisitions whose underlying motive is to prop up deteriorating performance of the acquiring company and rationalize the continued employment of its management group. There is evidence that suggests that the primary motivation for their acquisitions is increased prestige and standing in the business community.[1] When these combinations ultimately fail to produce results, the fact that corporate politics is often at the root of the problem receives very little mention.

Why do so many of these combinations take place if so many are doomed to failure?

---

[1] Judith Chevalier, Christopher Avery and Scott Shaefer, "Why Do Managers Undertake Acquisitions?" The Journal of Law, Economics and Organizations.

72

It's due to a very political instinct among corporate executives to extend their control over people and property beyond the limited confines of their own organization. The price of purchasing this additional control is called a premium. This premium, which is paid to the acquired company's owners, is commonly referred to as goodwill. The term goodwill is short for "go-ahead-against-your-will." That's because the acquired company's management knows that their interests will eventually be subordinated to those of the acquiring company's management. Therefore the amount of the acquisition premium is often in direct proportion to the amount of power - both economic and political - that they will be forced to relinquish.

Since, in two out of three cases, the premium paid goes beyond what the economics alone can justify, it should come as no surprise that the financial returns to the buyer are often unsatisfactory.

Recently, a number of business organizations have attempted to move away from this little-or-no-win situation in favor of a new business model that calls for the sharing of resources with other companies via partnerships and alliances. This new model flies directly in the face of the existing political model which advocates grabbing and holding. To the extent that the management of each organization can somehow set their politics aside in favor of this sort of mutual cooperation, the benefits to be gained are quite substantial.

To date, there has been limited success for the vast majority of these partnerships. The need to exercise undue influence over another organization's affairs is still predominant for most senior executives. The more political they are, the more they view a partnership as a cheap substitute for the complete control they would have with an outright acquisition.

Looking at the big picture, the quest for colonization has far from disappeared with the passing of the centuries. It has simply migrated from the realm of national governments to the realm of corporate governance.

But territory may no longer be the principal object of their desire. For today's power-mongers, there is a new source of corporate power that they simply cannot ignore.

This new source of power is information.

Information has recently been heralded as the new currency for the 21st century. Accordingly, substantial time and money has been invested in systems designed to do everything normally associated with currency, namely creating, warehousing, distributing and exchanging it.

What is new in the area of information is the trend towards sharing. Because information is so much like currency, it is very difficult for some people to get used to the idea of sharing it instead of hoarding it. From their point of view, why should they be required to share something of value without getting something in return?

The management gurus answer the question by suggesting that information is no different than any other company asset. Once acquired, it should be made freely available to those seeking to use it for the benefit of the organization.

This viewpoint is highly commendable from a business standpoint and equally contemptible from a political standpoint. Nothing is more contrary in nature to a corporate politician than an open and free exchange of information. It would be akin to allowing the trading of securities without requiring the payment of any commissions. In fact, for many who are politically predisposed, information is a form of security. With securities you rely on a brokerage system to regulate and measure the flow. The same holds true for information. As far as the politicos are concerned, getting information to the right people the right way at the right time is more important than getting the information right in the first place.

That is why the NACP (National Association of Corporate Politicians) has DIBS (Delicate Information Brokerage System) when it comes to handling information of a highly sensitive nature.

In theory, it is very similar to the way the NASD (National Association of Securities Dealers) uses its AQS (Automated Quotation System) to exchange up-to-date information about securities trades.

In practice, DIBS acts as a very secretive and segregated system designed to accomplish two key objectives:

1. Receive or exchange information that might prove valuable to political operatives in the organization.

2. Withhold any information that might prove damaging to political operatives in the organization.

Modern day proponents of knowledge management believe that no information of commercial value should ever be withheld from those who might be in a position to help the organization benefit from it. Despite these noble intentions, their efforts to expand the storehouse of management information have been continually bedeviled by obstructions in the supply line. Dumbfounded by these nagging problems with procurement and the resulting shortage of valuable inventory, these proponents of a free market for information have begun to beg the question...

WHO'S UNDERMINING THE STORE ?

An organization's store of information is never completely stocked with everything it needs, simply because a major portion of it is sequestered in the political nooks and crannies of the organization. Those responsible for withholding the information are generally waiting for the right time or place for it to be disclosed. The disclosure, if and when it does happen, almost always benefits those who withheld it.

The two basic kinds of information that politicians like to broker are:

1) Breakthrough information
2) Breakdown information

Breakthrough information is the kind that is most often derived from studying other organizations that utilize more advanced techniques. It can also be gleaned from studying the behavior of consumers who use a particular product or service. This information, once obtained, has the potential to introduce highly successful new products, services or ways of doing business into the organization.

Breakdown information is the kind you find buried deep inside the organization. It delves into all of the major problem areas of the business, namely products and services that don't sell, systems and processes that don't work, employees who aren't trained, etc. When this information becomes known, corrective actions are supposed to be taken to prevent those problems from hurting the organization.

The reasons why these two types of information are so sought after by the political elements are simple.

Breakdown information has the power to *fix* the business.
Breakthrough information has the power to *change* the business.

While there is plenty of other information circulating around the organization, the politicos and their information brokers know that these are the two that they need to pay the most attention to. That's because the discovery of break*down* information could suddenly expose failings, leading to a shift in the balance of power. Break*through* information could quickly disrupt the status quo by changing the course of the business.

If you're a politico in this sort of situation, you want to get DIBS on that kind of information before someone else does. If the information could ultimately prove harmful or embarrassing to someone in the organization, they want to make sure it isn't them.

However, in the fast-moving age of information, even the most savvy corporate politicians occasionally get caught with their proverbial pants down. It's usually because someone accidentally stumbled across some major discovery and broadcast it throughout the organization before the politicos had a chance to procure and broker it. When that happens, the politicos know the best way to diffuse the situation. They utilize a foil tactic that works as well in business as it does in politics.

It's known as...

THE POCKET VETO

Political leaders with a knack for using this device can undercut even the most revealing information without raising an eyebrow. Before they actually acknowledge the significance of the information, they proceed to take control of the assumptions that govern its usefulness. They decide what is relevant and what isn't relevant before the information is even considered. Those attempting to circumvent their approach, or introduce new ones, are accused of getting off track.

That was a lesson Frank learned the hard way. Frank wasn't a very subdued person by nature, which made him an easy target for this sort of accusation. Frank was the Director of Product Marketing for one of the nation's largest providers of household products and services. Faced with the prospect of declining sales due to cutthroat pricing by competitors, Frank had been putting together information on new distribution channels. His proposal, which was based on a considerable amount of research, was to package his company's products and services with those of another company in a related line of business. Packaged together, they could be distributed and discounted at less cost. To him, it was similar to packaging rental car reservations with airline reservations. It seemed like the kind of potential breakthrough that deserved some serious consideration.

Which is exactly why the company's EVP chose to sit on it. The EVP had a background in marketing strategy that had helped elevate him to his current position. It had been his idea to advertise at the national level and go after the mass market. This new approach had paid off handsomely over the last several years. Only recently had there been the problems with declining price levels and decreasing market share.

Frank's proposal represented a way to circumnavigate the competition and resolve those problems. It suggested an entirely new way to take the company's products and services to market. It raised the possibility of higher margins and market share. It even presented an opportunity to expand into global markets.

It also meant that the EVP, who had his eye on becoming CEO some day, was about to have his claim to fame staked by somebody else.

Faced with that possibility, the EVP had a different idea.

Presented with this compelling alternative during a staff meeting, the EVP steered Frank and his concept down a dead end street. When it was all over, Frank likened it to being taken on a tandem bike ride where the EVP sat in front and steered, and he was forced to sit in back and pedal blindly.

What the EVP did was take control of the "handle bars" that controlled where all of the questions and assumptions went during the discussion. Frank, on the other hand, had handle bars that were no good for anything except holding on for the ride. And go for a ride he did. Within minutes from the start of the meeting, the EVP started into a Q&A session with Frank about the marketing program. Rather than focus on the proposed program's strengths and weaknesses, he wanted to know if Frank had researched any ways to fix the current program.

Why was it having problems? Didn't it make more sense to fix the current program before undertaking a new one?

In no time, he had everyone else in the room ruminating on the current marketing strategy, rather than the new one that Frank proposed. By steering everyone towards the assumption that the current program was sound, but in need of some repair, the EVP succeeded in keeping the program he invented intact. He kept everyone answerable and accountable to his way of thinking about the business. In doing so, he neutralized Frank. Years later, when Frank eventually left for greener pastures, the company still had not implemented any variation on its existing marketing program, and was still looking for ways to stop the continuing decline in its margins.

When the situation eventually caught up with them years later, the company was suffering from ...

EXCESSIVE WAIT LOSS

This debilitating business condition is brought on by a persistent refusal to act quickly when a breakdown is uncovered or a breakthrough is discovered. The failure to respond often happens for all the wrong reasons, among them being...

- The need for a correction or the possibility of a breakthrough threatens a highly placed individual's political power and position in the company.

- An opportunity is identified by someone whose integrity is high but whose position isn't high enough to surmount the politics.

- Those at the root of the problem resist working on the solution until they can cover up the damage or shift the blame to another person or department.

At the end of the day, most of the critical information that a company needs to succeed is a knowledge of what will or won't work. The harder the proponents of knowledge management have tried to acquire it, the harder the politicos have tried to conceal it. The resulting stalemate has been mistakenly blamed on knowledge management techniques or technology. The blame actually rests with the information brokers who serve the politically-motivated parties in the organization. By deliberately stockpiling and dispensing information at their discretion, they manage to cheapen its real value.

CHAPTER SUMMARY

Unlike their counterparts in the pack, the colonials prefer to use far more subtle forms of conquest. Although they won't hesitate to fight for status in the organization, they are more interested in defending the status quo. It is their sacred cow. It represents the source of their strength.

But before they can defend the status quo, they have to define it. The way they go about doing so is to seize the earliest available opportunity to convince everyone that they hold the key to a brighter future. Using rhetoric that would be the envy of politicians everywhere, they garner the trust and confidence of their subordinates from the very outset. It's easy enough for them to do. Because people by nature want to trust those in authority, they usually give them the benefit of the doubt from the get-go.

Once they've turned this corner, they are free to impose their belief system on the rest of the organization. Unlike the situation in the pack environment where subordinates are afraid to think for themselves, people in the colonial environment are unwilling to think for themselves. The colony's leader is entrusted with the only key to the think tank. Everyone else eventually throws theirs away.

What the leaders build upon this foundation of trust is a house of cards from a marked deck. The substance of their leadership is a very rigid set of beliefs that prescribe what everyone else in the organization should accept as fact and fiction. Before any new ideas are taken seriously, they are filtered through this belief system to ensure they are consistent and supportive of it. Those who suggest ideas that aren't accommodating are sent on *a busyness trip* to get them out of sight and out of mind.

The belief systems that these leaders impose upon the rest of the organization are meant to be all-encompassing. That means no area is exempt from their edicts. Areas that resist are subject to takeover. The art of amassing outside functions under their span of control is second nature to them. Their way of conducting *business as use-u-all* is to take advantage of every person and every opportunity to broaden their empire.

With everyone anxiously looking over their shoulder to see if the leader's sights are set on them, less time is spent focusing on the needs of the business. As the rank and file start to realize that their managers care more about what the leaders think than what the customers think, apathy sets in. As customers begin to pick up on this apathy and respond in kind, these neglectful managers eventually find themselves *managing a work farce*. Before long, everyone starts getting into the act. To them, the game of "Follow The Leader" becomes easier to play than "Satisfy The Customer."

The leaders themselves are more than happy to invite these extra guests to the party. They promptly lay out the *WELCOME door mat*. It doesn't matter that some of these guests are less capable than others in taking care of business. Since those less capable of thinking and acting for themselves have a way of becoming more dependent and loyal, the leaders make a point of *working on the weakened* to help beef up their ranks. By promising them protection, and providing them with *duty-free gifts*, the leader can command unconditional support from this group. No matter how outrageous the request, no matter how injurious it might be to the organization, these followers-turned-zealots can be counted on to carry it out. Should things go wrong, and the need for help arise, the followers believe the leader will miraculously intervene in their *naiveté scene* and stay the consequences of their actions.

When the path to complete cooperation is periodically blocked by the occasional maverick, the leaders know how to deal with the adversity. Should a demand for a decision spring forth that threatens the status quo, they proceed to tackle the issue by using a divide and conquer strategy. Instead of short-circuiting the decision process, they draw it out endlessly by engaging multiple participants and opinions throughout the process. The constant frustration of having to entertain a steady stream of conflicting opinions leaves the decisionmakers dazed and thoroughly confused. This strategy for *winning by wearing down* helps discourage other would-be change agents from getting any ideas. It also serves to divide subordinates against themselves. Those whose ideas get defeated make the offenders pay *a penance for their thoughts*. It isn't long before all original thinking starts to die out.

With no new ideas around to threaten the status quo, the political elements can direct all of their energies towards expanding their *holey roamin' empire*. Those first to be targeted are areas outside the political leader's jurisdiction that have an annoying tendency to find problems within the leader's span of control. These leaders know that if they're not doing their own job well enough, it's time they did someone else's. The only caveat is, they get to do both yours and theirs. Those who choose not to take this threat seriously are due to be *delta coup d'etat*, and find themselves left behind as *the road-kill to success*. It usually doesn't become obvious until much later that the *error apparent* to the throne is basically unable to govern it judiciously. However, it is usually of little consequence due to the leader's ability to grant *diplomatic immunity* to those who end up losing control of their situation. The political leader's mutually-reinforcing circle of devotees helps insulate its members, but unfortunately not the organization, from any shortcomings.

When a leader's "quest for colonization" within an organization reaches its limit, or when they have bitten off more problems than they can eschew, it comes time for them to go in search of greener pastures. The greener grass is usually in the form of another organization. Knowing that the acquisition of another company will help shift attention away from difficulties of their own inside the organization, they go *looking for Mr. Good Bargain* at every opportunity. If they can succeed in bringing the management of an entire company under their control, they can use its people and property to further extend their influence and justify their own existence.

Although territory and subjects are a prized possession of the colonial ruler, nothing compares with their fixation on information. The most effective form of control available to a politician is exclusive knowledge of information. The private use of information to control perceptions of performance, particularly their own, is a critical advantage that they will not voluntarily relinquish. Given the chance, they will hoard it and refuse to share it with others until it suits their purpose. Those who go looking for it but are unable to access it are left to wonder *who's undermining the store* of information.

Every once in a while, some major piece of new information does slip past the politicos. In these rare instances, the politicians have another weapon at their disposal. If they cannot control the information, they control the way people think about it. Using very subtle forms of suggestion, they steer everyone down a path that leads to nowhere. Big ideas end up being reduced to passing thoughts that are of no consequence to anyone. Stripped of their significance, these once-promising pieces of information fall victim to *the pocket veto* and are ultimately discarded.

While all of this subterfuge is allowed to continue, the organization becomes increasingly incapable of correcting its shortcomings and recovering its losses. As customers grow more impatient and competitors grow more powerful, the foundation for the company's competitive advantage starts to crumble. If not promptly corrected, the result is *excessive wait loss* which, depending upon the amount of time elapsed, can be nearly impossible to recover from.

For those who find sanctuary in the shadow of leaders whose promises far exceed their results, the benefits prove to be short term. More often than not, the leaders move away in search of more abundant treasures, leaving their followers suddenly exposed and vulnerable. Sponsorless, they find themselves no longer able to contribute in a meaningful way. Most eventually fall victim to the higher standards of their leader's successor.

CHAPTER 5

CONSORTING WITH THE CLAN

Animals who gather together in clans are very territorial creatures who don't like staying in one place too long. Some species are incredibly opportunistic. Hyenas, for example, have offspring who will fight to the death even as they are coming into the world - just for the chance of becoming the "top dog".

They are known for their survival ability. They will feed on things that others have no stomach for. No matter how rancid it is, if it's available, they'll take it.

In the hunt, clans pursue large prey until it is exhausted. They then take advantage of its weakened condition by ganging up on it and taking it apart. Some, like Hyenas for instance, are better known for their scavenging ability - and for the evil cackling sound they make when excited by the prospect of a confrontation or a quick meal.

The loss of the Clan leader typically causes great anxiety amongst the group. There is generally chaos and a lot of infighting until a new leader takes over. Rival clans use this opportunity to try to take territory away from them.

In the corporate world, you're in a clan when you have a group of arrogant leaders half-heartedly trying to control a bunch of followers who are overly opportunistic and less willing to be dominated.

Among the less desirable characteristics of clans are:

Leaders with an inflated sense of self-importance who pay limited attention to followers.
Leaders who are very territorial in nature.
Followers who are highly opportunistic and confrontational.
Followers who are prone to infighting and one-upsmanship.

Instead of the heavy-handed tactics used by pack leaders, or the under-handed tactics used in colonies, the methods used by clan leaders can be best described as off-handed. The concept of regular communication with followers is foreign to them. Preoccupation with protecting their own territory precludes any meaningful dialogue with anyone outside of the leadership.

This separatist behavior on the part of the leadership engenders a high degree of isolation from the rest of the organization. As guardians of the territory entrusted to them, they steadfastly refuse to make room for any person or idea that might threaten their right of imminent domain. Their overwhelming desire to hold together their own empire leads them to behave in ways that are counterproductive for the organization.

- They withhold support for new initiatives that could help the company but would fall outside their span of control.

- They promptly criticize others after the first hint of a problem occurs in an area outside their jurisdiction.

- They immediately renounce allegiance to anyone who runs into trouble while acting on their behalf.

Their highly detached form of leadership engenders within the rank and file a similarly destructive breed of corporate politics.

When the practice of corporate politics extends to the rank and file, the resulting behavior resembles something straight out of a distorted version of The Good Book.   It's a bible that contains only three chapters.

Genesis
Exodus
Revelations

The book of Genesis proclaims that a career will be without form and void until one gets an invitation to the seniority prom. The only sure way to get that invitation and avoid being cut off from the top of the organization is to "get noticed." Getting noticed means bypassing one's immediate superiors whenever possible to endear oneself to someone higher up in the organization.

The book of Exodus teaches that a career cannot advance until one's adversaries are shown the door. It teaches disciples to make their way to the top of the organization after seeing to it that their fellow constituents are forced out. By draining the talent pool of legitimate contenders, those left standing tall in the shallow end can expect to be elevated to a higher position, should it ever become available.

The book of Revelations explains how to accomplish Genesis and Exodus. The use of revelations is something that politicians have turned into an exact science. In order to get noticed, they use revelations of previously undisclosed tidbits of information to gain access to their leader's sphere of influence. Once inside, they can elevate themselves to an even higher level by helping to solve problems or issues that potentially threaten their leader's span of control. These gratuitous offers of assistance typically win them regular access to the leader's inner sanctum. There, they can turn the opinions of the powers-that-be against their rivals.

The battles for supremacy engendered by this questionable code of conduct can wreak havoc on the morale and the motivation of a company's workforce. The extent of the damage that ensues depends upon the type of revelation made.

There are three types of revelations.

Level I - "I saw a scroll that was sealed"

Level II - "I saw a rider on a pale horse"

Level III - "I saw a great red dragon"

With the first type of revelation, the individual seeking to ascend the corporate ladder provides a higher-up in the organization with proprietary information about an issue or situation in the company. Although it may not be directed against any particular person, the fact that the information is currently unavailable to others in the organization gives the executive a distinct advantage. However, once the information gets disclosed outside of the proper channels, it can threaten the information broker with repercussions from those who get bushwhacked by it. The broker hopes that the information will ultimately prove to be of enough value to the higher up to shield them from these consequences. Therefore, to maximize the degree of secrecy, maintain the appearance of decency and achieve the element of surprise, everything has to be done very ...

HUSH-HUSH SWEET CHARLATAN

A classic example of this situation featured Dennis and Martin. For almost two years, Dennis had worked for Martin as his assistant manager of business planning and reporting. The two worked together like a pair of synchronized watches. Dennis always seemed to know exactly what Martin needed before he even had to ask. Martin knew what to expect from Dennis and allowed him a lot of leeway in making decisions.

Despite their difference in rank, Martin treated Dennis as an equal. Martin would frequently mention Dennis' outstanding performance to his superiors. It was his way of showing gratitude and giving credit where he believed credit was due.

This was fine as far as Dennis was concerned, but he had some secret ambitions that were not being fulfilled. For some time, he had been eyeing a position that reported to his boss's boss's boss who was a senior executive vice president and the number three person in the company. In his current position, Dennis saw no practical way of advancing to that level if he were to continue working his way up the ladder one rung at a time. What he desperately wanted was some hard and fast pull from the top to make it happen. All he needed was the right opportunity to hook up with a higher up so he could make his play.

The opportunity came when Dennis took advantage of a situation involving Martin. The company had recently experienced some downturn in performance and the pressure for faster earnings analysis and reporting had been steadily increasing. Martin, however, had been a bit slow in responding to this pressure. One day, Dennis got the opportunity to personally deliver one of the departmental reports directly to the senior executive vice president. When the executive reiterated the need for a much faster turnaround, Dennis was ready to jump at the chance.

"I know a way to get these reports out four days earlier if you're willing to accept a few estimates on some items," he suggested.

Pleasantly surprised by the go-getter mentality of this young lion, the executive suggested that Dennis provide him with an advance edition of the monthly reports, days before the final edition was released by Martin.

And that's exactly what Dennis did, without bothering to tell Martin.

Before long, Dennis was not only delivering the early edition, he was discussing it with the senior executive group. Rushed for time, the executives began asking Dennis for his own interpretation of the results. Dennis willingly obliged them. He also managed to put a little spin of his own into the explanations to make himself appear more knowledgeable.

Dennis pulled this off for as long as he could until Martin finally figured out what was going on. It happened when Martin went looking for his trusty sidekick to tell him about some last minute changes to the monthly numbers. Unable to locate him anywhere in the department, he asked one of the executive assistants if she had seen him.

"I believe he's in a meeting with the senior executive staff. I don't think they should be interrupted."

On the heels of this revelation, Martin questioned Dennis immediately afterwards.

"Were you ever going to get around to telling me about this little extracurricular activity of yours?" he asked.

"At this point, I don't really believe I owe you any kind of explanation," Dennis replied. "What I do for a senior executive of this company is their prerogative and it's not for you to question."

From that point on, Martin tried in vain to play down the increasing stature of his once-trusted aide. It soon became obvious that Martin was no longer in control. Dennis was taking all of his direction from the senior executive. Dennis' agenda began to supersede Martin's. Martin retaliated by trying to cut Dennis out of the loop, but his loop had shrunk to the point where it was too small and insignificant to bother Dennis.

Dennis was eventually promoted ahead of Martin. Martin remained behind in his current position until he eventually transferred to a different division of the company.

In the case of Martin and Dennis, the skirmish was limited to only two combatants. The struggle ended quickly and decisively with a few permanent injuries, but no major casualties.

Compared to what happens with the second sort of revelation, the previous situation was fairly civilized. The second revelation points to a rider on a pale horse. In organizational terms, that means taking aim at the manager of a department-in-distress. In the wake of the second revelation, the damage is more extensive. It usually causes at least one casualty when an unsuspecting comrade is victimized by someone close to them. That's the story behind the next feature entitled...

QUEST FOR FIRE-ING

There was once an organization that had an internal audit manager named Lewis. Lewis had been the company's manager of internal audit for several years. For quite some time, Lewis had been coveting the number two spot in the finance department. It was a V.P. Finance position that reported directly to the Chief Financial Officer.

One day, the incumbent V.P. of Finance was transferred to another division and the position became available. Unfortunately for Lewis, the person appointed to the position was the accounting manager. This accounting manager had only been with the company for 18 months. However, she had somehow managed to catch the eye of the CFO as a result of her involvement in some successful expense reduction projects.

What made things even worse for Lewis was the fact that he had helped her along during that entire time. Believing it would endear him to the CFO, he had helped her get up to speed during her orientation period. He had also refrained from reporting on some deficiencies in her accounting area, choosing instead to downplay the issues in hopes that it would keep controversy to a minimum, and his chances for promotion to a maximum.

Any pretense of loyalty to the new V.P. completely disappeared the day Lewis was passed over for his coveted position. Before the new V.P. could solidify her position, Lewis figured he would dig for anything he could find to promptly discredit her and get her removed from the job that he believed was rightfully his.

In his position as manager of internal audit, Lewis knew where all the bodies were buried. He was privy to problems in the accounting department that existed long before the new accounting manager had arrived. He also knew that the time spent by the accounting manager on the CFO's expense reduction projects had kept her from dealing with those problems in a timely manner. Lewis knew that the problems were in areas that were highly sensitive in nature and would be very difficult for her to explain away.

The very next internal audit report that Lewis promptly issued made it a point to expose those problems and expound upon their many repercussions. The content was quite damaging and the tone highly accusatory. The new V.P. was caught off guard. She spent the next several months responding to inquiries from the company's outside auditors. The parent company became increasingly concerned as Lewis continued to release a barrage of disparaging reports from internal audit. The parent company was eventually forced to intervene.

The official casualty list read as follows:

The CFO's career path to a higher position at the parent company was permanently blocked.

The V.P. of Finance voluntarily transferred to a position of lesser responsibility in a different division, in lieu of resigning.

The internal audit manager was promoted and later terminated for lack of performance.

In this case, the people in finance made a huge mistake by assuming that the higher ups in the organization would somehow intercede and stabilize a situation that was getting out of hand. When these sorts of situations crop up in a clan type of environment, the leaders don't really care who comes out ahead or without a head. As long as the conflict doesn't pose an immediate threat to themselves, they gladly indulge such behavior for as long as it takes to declare a winner and expel a loser. Why? Because they know that the winner's triumph is conditional. They know that a rank and file member cannot uphold their victory unless they pay homage to preserve their ill-gotten gain.

However, if a situation does pose an immediate threat to a clan leader, they will swiftly intervene on their own behalf. It is their response to this third and most threatening revelation of a great red dragon that stirs them to use every means necessary to protect themselves.

The great red dragon in this case is a fellow executive whose conduct is disrespectful of the status quo. Fellow executives who willfully disregard set boundaries and repeatedly cross the line are a menace to the political order. These dragons must be immediately expunged from the kingdom in order to keep everything on a safe and even keel.

The dragonslaying urge is particularly keen when political leaders have problems of their own to deal with. During their unwelcome meanderings across the corporate landscape, dragons have an annoying tendency to stumble across shortcomings in other's domains. Once discovered, these deficiencies could be used by a dragon to shift the balance of power in their favor. To keep that from happening, politicians promptly go on the offensive.

With near-religious fervor, they assemble their armies to lead against the foe. They know if they can succeed in sacrificing the dragon, they can shift the blame for their own shortcomings onto it and appease the angry gods of underperformance. Into this army they frequently recruit members of the rank and file. Betty was one such recruit. When the CEO of a large auto parts distributor saw the company's performance pushing him closer to the chopping block, he needed a dragon to slay... and fast. In this case, it was the COO who was the perfect sacrifice. But it couldn't be done without first finding some plausible proof of misdoing.

That's where Betty came in. As purchasing manager for the company, she knew all about the corporate "comings and goings" of both the good and bad variety. The CEO figured that with her help, he could stitch together a case, tie up a few loose ends and make his COO look the part for his upcoming role in...

PRETTY IN PINK-SLIP

The COO in Betty's company was the kind of person who became easily frustrated by any sign of bureaucratic resistance. Several of his new policy initiatives had either been delayed or implemented too slowly for his liking. To move things along faster, he had resorted to implementing several major changes in the business without fully informing the CEO or anyone else affected by the changes. While these changes were intended to improve the situation, they were not always popular with the rank and file.

Betty was one of the first to experience this discontent. Her responsibility for purchasing put her in frequent contact with other managers in the company, managers who were often infuriated about not being consulted or informed about major changes. Although these failures in communication were not directly responsible for the recent downturn in the company's performance, in the minds of some, they did constitute sufficient cause for alarmists.

When the CEO approached Betty for information, it was the first time he had ever done so. His general unwillingness to fraternize with the troops was legendary in the organization. So surprised and flattered was Betty by his sudden show of interest that she told him everything she had ever heard about the COO, including the fact that several managers considered him a few fries short of a happy meal. While Betty couldn't say for sure if she was ultimately responsible for what happened next, it took less than two months for the CEO to secure the resignation of the COO, thereby securing his own position as CEO and "Acting COO."

In Betty's case, she got worked over by a very cunning and politically astute leader of the organization. In these types of situations, few if any can resist the urge to spill their guts. However, in the highly opportunistic clan environment, this sort of inducement isn't always necessary. More times than not, members of the rank and file will secretly volunteer damaging information about an unpopular executive in hopes that it will get them ousted. This mutinous act earns the perpetrators admiration for their award-winning performance as the

PIRATES OF PENSIONS

Those victimized by these renegade acts are executives who choose to act solely in the company's interests and consider themselves safely beyond the reach of corporate politics. They storm into organizations with noble intentions to turn things around on a dime by restructuring here, downsizing there, divesting this, acquiring that, and so on and so forth. These would-be heroes set themselves up to be easy targets for grass-roots politicians who know what will and will not be tolerated by the people in the trenches. It generally comes as no surprise to anyone except the soon-to-be-former executive when (s)he gets hit by

THE B.U.S.

The B.U.S. is short for **B**lindsider of **U**nsuspecting **S**capegoats.

This particular B.U.S. is owned and operated by the P.O.R.T. (Political Operatives Rapid Transit) Authority and service is available to every organization in America. However, this is not the kind of B.U.S. people ride in.

It's the kind they get thrown under.

When someone gets hit by this BUS, their career is killed instantly. The only clue they have that it's coming is the distance their peers suddenly start keeping from them. A victim's only recourse is to sprawl helplessly at the base of the corporate ladder and beg for alms for the blind-sided.

This kind of treatment, no matter how unfair or unfortunate, plays right into the hands of the remaining leadership. Immediately following the departure of these would-be icons of the company, an autopsy ensues. During this autopsy, which can last for months or even years, the dearly departed get blamed for just about everything that went wrong while they were there. They also get blamed for things that went wrong well before they arrived and long after they left. A "coroner's report" officially absolves all those remaining in power of any wrongdoing. From deep within the political circles of the company, the message goes forth...

"Performance problems are caused by those who leave. The leftovers are never at fault."

This ingenious maneuver leaves everyone believing that those who try to change things are untrustworthy, and that those who manage to prevent it are deserving of sainthood.

This highly suspect behavior on the part of senior management does not mean that all political backstabbing is the result of some high level conspiracy. On the contrary, most knifing victims either provoke these attacks upon themselves or self-inflict their own injuries - with no help at all from anyone else.

Those who provoke attacks upon themselves are often very trustworthy people who naively assume that everyone else is cut from the same cloth. By steadfastly refusing to acknowledge the presence of politics in the corporate landscape, they feel perfectly free to acknowledge their own errors and shortcomings. In doing so, they sidle up to the political ticket window and offer to pay...

THE HIGH PRICE OF ADMISSION

Corporate politics is particularly cruel to those who have an overly developed sense of right and wrong. That's because they have an annoying tendency to admit rather than cover up their mistakes.

When a mistake is made and admitted, an organization is spared the time that gets wasted trying to find another plausible explanation for the problem(s) it caused. While the ostensible purpose of this noble gesture is to clear the conscience of the mistake-maker, it also has the effect of ringing the dinner bell. It kick-starts a ritual within the political circles known as

The **F.E.E.D.**

The F.E.E.D. stands for **F**renzy to **E**xpose **E**rroneous **D**eeds. In the world of corporate politics, before you graciously serve up your mistakes on a silver platter, you have to do a hunger-check first. If you volunteer fresh meat to a bunch of success-starved political operatives, you can expect your admission to be served up countless times for continuous consumption. It's not necessarily because someone has it in for you. It's because you helped them balance a very important political equation that states:

One mistake of yours in hand = Three of theirs in the bush

When a business situation becomes politically charged, the revelation of one isolated mistake can become the oft-repeated explanation for a variety of problems.

97

Jim never dreamed that was possible. Until he met Hank.

Jim was the Planning Manager for a large equipment leasing company. His responsibilities included preparing revenue and expense projections to ensure that the Equipment division's profit objectives would be achieved. Having spent most of his career handling similar responsibilities for a variety of companies, he had learned that no set of projections could ever be perfect. Therefore, he always managed to build some "insurance" into his projections to compensate for any that might be off the mark. This approach helped his Division achieve its profit objectives year after year even when it underperformed in a couple of categories.

Then one day Jim got a new boss named Hank. Hank was transferred in from the parent company's headquarters to become the new CFO. The former CFO, with whom Jim had had a very good working relationship, had taken early retirement at age 55.

With his new boss in place, Jim continued to prepare the upcoming year's plan projections the same way he always did. Responding to pressure from the CEO for more aggressive growth in new customer sales, the division managers turned in some highly optimistic revenue goals. Seeing that these revenue projections would be particularly hard to achieve, Jim built some cushion into the expense projections. He figured the extra provision in the expenses would help counterbalance any difficulties the sales managers might have in achieving their revenue goals.

But things turned out differently. Thanks to a series of ill-conceived cost cutbacks that had been made in the sales and service departments in previous years, customers were starting to suffer from a steady decline in the speed and quality of service. Many of these customers threatened to take their business elsewhere unless the service level improved dramatically. Suddenly the division was having to play catch-up. It was hiring more sales and service people than planned - at a higher than expected starting wage. Compounding these problems was the shortfall in sales revenue that Jim had anticipated. In spite of his carefully placed cushions, the Equipment Division began to fall short of its profit goal for the first time in ten years.

Unlike his predecessor, the CFO was too new to the company to find a quick fix for the problem. The CEO was getting increasingly agitated by the situation. It was time for someone to own up for the shortfall, and, not surprisingly, there was a noticeable lack of volunteers.

A series of senior management "shampoo" meetings ensued (the kind where everyone gathers, tenses and repeats). The CFO was in desperate need of an explanation to give the parent company. No one wanted to admit that the earlier decision to cut costs had backfired. So Jim made the mistake of trying to help everyone out by admitting he thought the revenue projections in the plan were overly optimistic.

"So you think the plan may have been the problem?" asked Hank.

"I would say it was definitely part of it," admitted Jim.

Jim didn't bother to explain that he had put expense cushions in the plan to cover the revenue shortfall. Since the expenses had already ended up higher than planned, he figured it wasn't worth mentioning.

When a report was finally issued to the parent company, Jim sat down to read it. On the first page were Hank's list of explanations for the unfavorable profit variance. Prominently displayed at the top of the list was the number one reason:

"Errors made by the Planning group in estimating sales revenues were the principal cause of the shortfall."

Needless to say, Jim's relationship with his new boss, and his reputation with the parent company weren't all that good after that.

An even more amazing aspect of corporate politics is that you don't necessarily have to admit mistakes in order to have them thrown back in your face. Sometimes, because of some error in the distant past, a person can suddenly become the convenient target for a full exposé. There is no protocol in the political playbook that requires anyone to tell the unsuspecting victim ...

"YOUR SLIP-UP IS SHOWING"

At least no one did that for Jim's former boss, which is why he ended up becoming a former boss. When he took early retirement at age 55, it wasn't voluntary; it was mandatory. His choice was to either retire or be terminated. He elected the former.

The strange thing about it was, at the time of his "retirement", the former CFO was considered by virtually everyone in the company to be extremely competent, reliable and hard-working. Most agreed that his performance over the last ten years was exemplary.

When the decision was made to replace him, the question of his ability never entered the picture. The event was ultimately triggered by some special agenda that was being followed somewhere higher up in the organization. The intent in most cases is to bring about a changing of the guard. When someone's position happens to be the turnkey, the "architects of overthrow" often don't need to do much to discredit them, and the opportunity is always there. Their methods range anywhere from the extremely subtle to the incredibly blatant.

In the case of Jim's former boss, the parent company had become uncomfortable with the way he was handling certain issues. It wasn't that he was doing an unsatisfactory job. His priorities just weren't the same as theirs.

At the same time, the parent company had several individuals in its own accounting function whose orientation was more along the lines of what they wanted to have in place at the subsidiary level.

When both motive and opportunity exist simultaneously, all it takes is for someone somewhere high up in the chain of command to issue a simple and unmistakable directive:

"Remove Tab A; Insert Tab B"

Jim's boss was Tab A. So he was history.

Hank was Tab B. So he became the new CFO.

Those in a position to support Jim's boss were faced with a real dilemma. Should they stand behind him on principle and risk being run over by the same B.U.S.? Or should they simply step back and hope he'd land safely on his feet somewhere else?

In the end, the answer was obvious. People who possess above-average survival skills know full well that it's better to steer clear of these confrontations than to risk falling into...

THE PARENT-COMPANY TRAP

Many of those who have risen to a high-level position of authority in an organization will tell you, "It's not how you *start* that counts, but how you *finish*."

If you probe a little deeper, you'll get the real story. It's not *how* you start that counts, but *where*.

There is always more than one path to the top, just as there are multiple running lanes on a track. The big difference is, not everyone in the running gets the same start. Whenever someone from the corporate office enters the race, it behooves those running next to them to know how handicapped they are before sprinting flat out towards the finish line.

According to the rules of corporate politics, a runner is handicapped if:

1. They joined the company from outside the organization.
2. They never worked at the company's headquarters.

When attempting to outrun the competition, it is always better to be a card-carrying, dues-paying member of the establishment. The establishment is that enviable entourage of people at the corporate headquarters whose faces are usually pointed in the direction of the corner office, and whose backsides are usually pointed directly towards you. These are the people whose vote of confidence gives a runner the inside track. Challengers who come from outside the organization do not impress these people, no matter how fast or how far they can sprint. They generally don't pay attention to anyone who hasn't paid their dues.

The dues are the kind paid to them during an extended tour of duty in their "Fortress of Servitude" (a.k.a. corporate headquarters). In order to push your way into the inner circle, you have to kiss your way past a lot of backsides. Once this dirty dues-paying work is done, you come away with some very powerful allies at the highest levels of the organization, allies whose influence can put you in play almost anywhere in the entire organization and keep you there for as long as it suits their purpose.

Their purpose is simple. Influence. Once you've been indoctrinated into their way of doing things, you become their influence peddler. You end up instilling their corporate mindset into everyone you come into contact with. If you see things going in such a way that would upset HQ, you have a direct line to them that you can use without fear of reprisal. As a card-carrying, dues-paid member, you are entitled to all the rights and special privileges pertaining thereto. If anyone outside of HQ tries to mess with you, they do so at their own peril.

Which is why the comrades of Jim's former boss scattered like roaches under a floodlight. They didn't want the heel of HQ to land on them as it closed in on him.

In the tumultuous world of clan politics, it isn't always one person who is victimized. There are cases in which multiple battle lines are drawn between hordes of zealots who pit themselves against each other in the relentless pursuit of conquest. When that happens, the behavior enters a whole new realm. It can take the form of a running gun-battle between groups who dislike each other. Or sometimes it can be the result of a bitter breakup over some major disagreement, one that leads from the way of peaceful coexistence to...

THE WAY WE WAR

Love-hate relationships do not exist solely in the private world after business hours. There are plenty of these made-for-Jerry-Springer altercations going on between the hours of eight and five. The one event that most often triggers these disputes is a change of leadership. Specifically, two groups who used to report to one person will end up reporting to separate people. When the single force that held them together is suddenly split in two, all kinds of repressed hostility erupt.

The earliest casualties from these hostilities are the people in Group A who mistakenly believe that their former comrades in Group B will nobly resist any urge to advance beyond their separate turf. Most casualties occur while members of the A team are resting peacefully in the naive notion that their status in the new commonwealth is absolutely safe and secure.

Nothing could be further from the truth.

A division of leadership between two departments invariably results in a redrawing of the lines that separate them. This presents the more opportunistic members of each group with a perfect excuse to capitalize on the vulnerabilities of their former brethren. In pursuit of

103

their next promotion, they will gladly exchange loyalty for license. Armed with once-secret information about who can do this and who can't do that, they start moving in on territory that they know belongs to members of their former peer group.

Jerry got a taste of that first hand.

Jerry was the Manager of Marketing for a large retailer of men's apparel. Jerry and his group reported to the Vice President of Marketing and Sales at the company's headquarters. Also reporting to the Vice President was Jerry's counterpart Tracy who was Manager of the Catalog Sales Division. During the time they both reported to the V.P., Tracy's group would routinely share information about competitor pricing and promotions with Jerry's marketing people. The information was extremely valuable because it came directly from customers who were calling the company's central 800 telephone number to compare prices and purchase items from the catalog. Tracy's people were always the first to learn about changes in the competition from their conversations with customers. By passing this information on to marketing, Jerry's group was able to respond quickly with new advertising and new offers.

There was regular interaction between the two groups. Whether it was lunch hour or happy hour, you'd find them socializing together. And that's exactly the way it was until Tracy's group was reassigned to a different executive following a merger with another retailer. As a result of the merger, a new Vice President of National Sales position was created and Tracy's catalog division was realigned under it.

Tracy figured that her position in Catalog sales put her in an ideal position to get a promotion she had been secretly longing for.

Unbeknownst to Jerry, she began to mobilize a few key people in the catalog division. Together, they launched a campaign to wrest control of a major portion of the marketing budget away from Jerry. By enlarging the Catalog budget at the expense of marketing, Tracy hoped to print more catalogs more frequently. This would give her more control over what the company offered. It would also steer more customer traffic to the Catalog division, thereby enriching her annual bonus, which was based on a percentage of its sales volume.

Tracy's first act of aggression was to sever Jerry's supply lines. Her people stopped forwarding any competitor information they received from customers. Without it, Jerry's advertising became less competitive. Tracy's next hostile act was to inform her new boss of problems with the company's advertising agency. These problems, which Jerry was in the process of resolving, were construed by Tracy to be a sign of weakness on the part of Jerry's account managers. She and her people were ultimately able to convince their new boss that the best solution would be a budgetary shift from marketing to sales. Jerry's account managers ended up taking a twenty percent cut in their national advertising budget. The money was allocated to a new local advertising department that reported to the catalog division.

With all of that increased responsibility, the catalog division needed a higher ranking individual at the Director level. The short list of candidates included.

1. Godzilla
2. Attila the Hun
3. Tracy

This sort of gut-wrenching story about love and betrayal pales in comparison to the ringside experience you get when two groups have no love lost for one other. When these combatants pit themselves against each other, the result is the sort of serious bloodletting you witness when you watch...

RAGING BULL _ _ _ _

In the world of corporate politics, those given to telling tales of misfortune about others in order to get ahead often find it difficult to limit their practice to individual character assassinations only. In their eagerness to impress their leaders, many will not hesitate to instigate major warfare among entire groups of their own peers. The resulting infighting serves a dual purpose. First, it keeps their fellow members of the rank and file off balance and in a continually defensive posture. Second, in the midst of all the turmoil, it allows them to stand safely aside and officiate the contest, helping the powers-that-be achieve their desired outcome.

That's exactly what happened when the consumer and commercial divisions of a major equipment dealer took each other on in a departmental duel to the death.

The business of the company was the sale, installation and servicing of a variety of heating, ventilation and air conditioning (HVAC) equipment. In this highly political organization, success was more often measured by the size of one's department and less often by its accomplishments. Nobody's territory was safe from invasion. That was mostly due to Jeffrey and his commercial services group. In his quest to create a world-class service organization, he had managed to double the size of the commercial division despite the fact that business in general was growing at a much slower rate. He had accomplished this rather amazing feat by "annexing" as many other departments as he could. His approach was simple and very effective. Using an always popular governmental construct known as "manifest destiny", Jeffrey set about convincing the higher-ups that customers would be better served by one all-encompassing service organization, not a series of individually specialized functions. The advancement of this theory was the backbone of Jeffrey's political maneuvering. His approach seemed to make logical sense because, like any other political statement of position, it had never been extensively road-tested in the real world of business. Before anyone else could get around to figuring that out, Jeffrey would make his move and overtake another department. Within two years, he had gained control of three major departments in the company. No one in the executive group ever bothered to investigate the considerable problems he was having in absorbing all those groups into his organization.

Jeffrey's moment of truth came when he set his sights on the consumer services division. This area had the responsibility for scheduling service on equipment installed in homes. It was also responsible for handling customer billing and billing-related issues.

From Jeffrey's point of view, the consumer services group was not measuring up from a customer service mentality. For one thing, they didn't stay open as late as the commercial division. They also didn't have people answering every call; instead they frequently used automated answering machines. As far as he was concerned, they weren't doing everything possible to keep the customer satisfied.

Jeffrey concluded that the consumer division could become more customer-responsive by combining it with his own operations. By doing so, he figured he could make it more cost-effective as well. However, in this latest attempt at conquest, he ran up against his fiercest opposition.

Eleanor.

Eleanor was no novice to the ways of Jeffrey, and she wasn't buying any of his untested theories that called for a merger of the two divisions. As manager of the consumer group for more than eight years, she had witnessed some serious lack of precision in the way things were handled in Jeffrey's organization. She believed adamantly that turning over the consumer division to Jeffrey would result in a lot of incorrectly handled accounts.

Eleanor's refusal to capitulate was something Jeffrey wasn't accustomed to. His previous conquests had required very little arm twisting. Just a few objections to overcome and it was usually his for the taking. With Eleanor, he was up against the manager of a function that didn't particularly need or want his help. For the first time ever in the eyes of his superiors, Jeffrey was facing some fairly serious opposition.

Realizing that Eleanor's position of strength was the obstacle, Jeffrey set out to eliminate it. To do so, he needed to find some weaknesses in her area that he could use to his advantage. What followed was a grass-roots defamation campaign conducted by the employees of commercial division against the employees in consumer. Telephone records were secretly obtained and disclosed to Eleanor's superiors. Some angry letters from customers complaining about the way their problems were handled were used to incriminate people in the consumer group. By skimming over the fact that many of the problems were isolated events, this tactic managed to put Eleanor's people on the defensive. Accusations started to fly between the two groups, followed by some nasty telephone exchanges.

"You might as well quit now because you'll never get a job working for us when we take you over," said the people in commercial.

"You've got your own business so screwed up, you'll never get the chance to destroy ours too," replied consumer.

After months of these types of exchanges, morale was so low in Eleanor's area that people started leaving. They either defected to the commercial side to protect their job or they left the company altogether. The department's performance suffered to such an extent that Jeffrey was eventually able to absorb its remnants, ostensibly to prevent any further decline in performance.

So how did it all turn out?

Jeffrey's unwelcome advances towards the other departments had netted him the single largest area of responsibility in the entire company. His group was now responsible for over six separate and distinct functions, each with their own unique set of issues. Unfortunately, Jeffrey hadn't counted on the fact that consumers had different service expectations than the commercial customers. Their billing issues were more numerous and difficult to resolve.

Nevertheless, Jeffrey had to pare down the combined staff in order to achieve the cost reductions he had promised to deliver. Service representatives were required to handle both consumer and commercial customer issues. It wasn't long before the pressures of handling so many different sets of demands culminated in the loss of some key individuals in those functions. Their departure resulted in a veritable freefall in performance. It wasn't until this final scene in the continuing drama unfolded that the company came to realize...

HOW THE WORST WAS WON

In the final analysis, Jeffrey's politics turned out to be far more convincing than his performance. All of the "territory" he had amassed in his empire became increasingly difficult to govern. Managers who had been used to handling routine issues in a specific area were unable to keep up with the increasing demands made on them by the new array of customers.

In keeping with the code of clan politics, Jeffrey was ultimately able to shift the blame for his deteriorating performance onto those whose areas he had overtaken.

Also keeping to the code of the clan, the leadership of the company stood back and did nothing to stop the fracas that Jeffrey's politics had caused. They excused themselves and the poor performance in general by dismissing them as nothing more than "workout issues" related to a change in the customer service culture. Their rationalization of this bad behavior allowed Jeffrey and others like him to wage his "attack and attach" campaign across the organization, leaving morale in shambles in its wake. As the integrity and stability of one area after another was compromised by this sort of ritualistic ambush, the employees stopped working together in a single-minded fashion. Instead, they started to separate into smaller social circles, known as cliques. The cliques helped restore some sense of safety, confidence and purpose that they lost when their leaders left them vulnerable to attack. In these tiny clans, the wagons were always circled.

In cliques, conversation centers upon the weaknesses of those outside the circle. The prospect of an all-out war keeps everyone constantly vigilant for any sign of aggressive behavior inside or outside their own area. If spotted, they promptly respond with a massive amount of angry saber-rattling, no matter how small or insignificant the threat. Eventually, enough people become so defensive that the company can no longer focus on the business at hand.

This widespread rash of soreness and blurred vision are the first unmistakable signs that the organization has suffered the ill-effects of a major

STAFF INFECTION

It doesn't matter how healthy any area may have been in the past. All are susceptible to this sort of illness if the germ(inator) is allowed to spread out into the working environment. As was true in Jeffrey's case, if it radiates out far enough, a malignant atmosphere sets in. As the disease spreads, the clear line of sight that people once had towards the organization's goals and objectives gets more and more obstructed. People turn from acting on the issues to acting out their own aggressions. As William Butler Yeats put it, " The center does not hold; things fall apart."

Because the disease can spread so quickly, the only way to stop it is to prevent it from circulating in the first place. Prevention requires routine checkups from the company's caretakers (i.e. its leaders). Early intervention becomes critical once an infection is discovered.

Clan politics breeds the kind of leaders who withhold this treatment when its need is most critical. That was certainly true in the case of Stewart. By failing to act in time to stop the infection, he not only hurt his own department, he became hazardous to the health of an entire organization.

Stewart was the executive in charge of information technology services for a large machine parts distributor. Unlike his predecessors. Stewart had a reputation for being very hands off when it came to the management of his department. The only problems he would bother to deal with personally were those brought to him by the president of the company. He expected the managers in his department to solve their own problems without having to turn to him for help.

Stewart had been in charge for almost a year when the company acquired another distributor whose headquarters were located in the same city. As a result of the acquisition, Stewart inherited another information systems (I.S.) department. Unlike the members of his own staff, this newly acquired department was using a newer type of computer system. The technology represented the latest advances in mainframe computing and Stewart was eager to see how well it actually worked.

Over the next few months, Stewart focused almost exclusively on the new technology. He spent considerable time at the acquired company's facilities trying to identify potential applications of the newer technology in his own organization. His new I.S. department interpreted Stewart's interest to mean that he was eventually going to convert everyone to it. Back in Stewart's headquarters, his own people were beginning to dread the same thing. When it finally came time for the two groups to move in together under the same roof, the program, you might say, erred out.

It wasn't long before the acquired company's programmers began hesitating to help Stewart's people on projects involving the old technology. The old technology, they argued, was destined to be dumped in favor of their newer technology. Not only would the old technology be replaced, but those who used it as well.

111

Needless to say this did not sit well with the people in Stewart's group. Confronted with this difference of opinion, they looked to Stewart for resolution. But Stewart didn't want the problem. Rather than deal with it, he elected to keep his options open and allow the conflict in his department to continue unabated. Believing this would buy him time to make a decision, Stewart gave no indication as to which side of the fence he was going to come down on.

Stymied by this complete lack of decisiveness, the two groups continued to undermine each other, going so far as to spread their private war out into other areas of the company. They began soliciting support from people in other departments. Threats and accusations were traded back and forth on such a regular basis that they became an expected part of the daily regimen. But the threat of job loss was more than most could take for very long. As the new technology group eventually began to convince the old technology group that Stewart's abstinence constituted a decisive vote in their favor, the resignations started to climb. Not until his own group was nearly decimated was Stewart finally forced to intervene. By then it was too late to recover. Although he still had many of the company's computer programs running on the old technology, he had lost the people who knew how to run them and maintain them.

Plans to convert over to the new technology had to be dealyed or permanently postponed due to the resulting absence of expertise on the old system.

In situations such as these, when embattled employees find themselves faced with a persistent unwillingness by the leadership to intervene, the rank-and-file members of the "clan" seek an alternate outlet for their pent-up frustration. Separate factions will unite in order to seek greater influence. If a high level management position comes up for grabs, these factions will pull themselves together on a temporary basis and do whatever it takes to make sure that someone sympathetic to their cause gets elected. The way they go about doing that is to form a f.a.m.i.l.y. - a fearsome amalgamation of malcontents, insurgents, libelers and yahoos. The next official act of these family members is to target their opposition and form

THE DISCREDIT UNION

The kind that William got to experience first hand. When his company made the decision to consolidate three of its operating departments into a single department for cost saving purposes, William was the odds-on favorite to be selected as its manager. Having served in one of the three departments being merged, he had amassed an admirable track record and reputation for integrity in that area. Although he wasn't as well known in the other two departments, his experience with the company and his knowledge of its policies and procedures was considerably greater than any of the other candidates. Throughout the inner circles of the company, his name kept coming up as the first choice for the new position.

Those in favor of William were convinced he was the most qualified in terms of knowledge and experience.

Those opposed to William knew that he was better qualified than anyone else. They also knew that his button-down, no-nonsense approach would lead him to act quickly, decisively and, in a word, apolitically. Knowing that William would not allow himself to be influenced by extraneous interests, many feared he would refuse to "close ranks" with them, meaning he could not be relied upon to use any of the power of his new position to help them advance into the upper echelons of the organization. The prospect of being deprived of that kind of influence is something that a true politician won't accept without a fight.

The best place for them to wage such a fight is the realm of public opinion. They begin by convening unofficial tribunals in the hallways and doorways. Their express purpose is to find everything that can be used to derail any "undesirables" aspiring to higher office. If something of value surfaces, it is quickly and discreetly pushed upstairs to the decisionmakers. Sometimes it's a pointed question, such as "Are we prepared to accept a less customer-friendly approach if we install some hard-nosed engineer in that position?" Other times, it's a generic comment such as "I'm not sure the best solution to this problem is someone who may have no potential beyond this position."

In William's case, the politicos had a tough sell on their hands. Here was a guy who possessed everything he needed in terms of competence and credibility. He had proven time and time again that he could get results. Anyone trying to attack him from the integrity angle was in for an uphill battle.

William's opposition knew that to win, they would have to put his business philosophy on trial instead of his credentials. To help steer the debate in that direction, they resorted to one of the more popular and successful methods for steering public opinion in their favor. In football circles it's known as the misdirection play. The misdirection play is designed to convince everyone on the opposing side to react a certain way - a way which leads them in the wrong direction, away from the true course of the play. In business, the object is to fool everyone on the opposite side of an issue into thinking about it the wrong way. Politicians know that wrong thinking inevitably leads people to the wrong conclusion.

And in William's case, it worked perfectly.

To direct the decisionmakers' thinking away from the issues of competence and credibility, William's opponents substituted his degree of open-mindedness and willingness to function as a team player. His background in one of the three departments, once considered an asset, now resembled a liability. Did he fully understand the big picture? Was he too one sided or narrow-minded in his thinking?

What eventually managed to seep to the top of the organization, and into the minds of the decisionmakers, was that William was too pragmatic and idealistic for a position of such importance. What was needed was a conceptual thinker with a knack for doing things in ways that were far more innovative than anything William had ever attempted. That meant appointing a recently hired assistant manager from one of the company's service departments. This assistant manager had already demonstrated a willingness to take risks by using cross-training methods that were highly innovative, almost speculative in nature. The decisionmakers believed that any wrinkles that might develop during the transition could always be "ironed out" later.

The decision eventually cost the company millions of dollars in lost business, because it violated a basic business principle that states:

"If it doesn't wash, it won't iron out."

William knew that the tasks to be performed in the combined area would be highly technical and not conducive to cross-training. Nevertheless, the new appointee proceeded to superimpose that approach on top of the specialized functions. The employees were quickly overwhelmed by the array of complex tasks they were required to perform. They quit in droves, leaving those left behind with an even tougher job. Meanwhile, customers got frustrated with the breakdown in service and discontinued doing business with the company.

The "starch" reality was - it was too big a problem to iron out.

Misdirection is not the only method available when it becomes necessary to sabotage an opponent's career aspirations. Long before any opportunity for advancement comes along, the politically astute will resort to another subversive maneuver to disqualify their opposition. Reminiscent of the proverbial smear campaign, it's known as...

TALKING ON THE TELL-A-PHONY LINE

There is a timeless truth in politics that states "Perception is Truth". Those who are savvy to this age-old truth know that an uninformed opinion can be just as effective as a factual representation. These people believe when the opportunity knocks, never tell anyone where the truth "lies".

This is the tactic most often employed when character assassins need ammunition. By the time the victim realizes they've been hit, the damage is beyond repair.

That's what happened in Alice's case. Alice was the manager of acquisitions for a financial services company. Since joining the company, she had been striving to obtain a senior management position with responsibility for the company's lending operations. Recognizing that the company lacked a dependable system for credit scoring new loan customers, she had been developing a unique set of standards and statistics to evaluate high risk customers during the lending decision process. The knowledge she had acquired had proven very helpful during recent acquisitions of loan portfolios. Her expertise was starting to become noticed and even sought after by some of the personnel in the lending operations.

Unfortunately for her, one of the managers in the loan department was none too happy with Alice's increasing celebrity status. This manager, whose name was Edward, had been in the loan department for more than six years. He had been frequently passed over for promotions. His level of frustration had continued to mount as newcomers into the department routinely passed him by on their way to senior management positions. Although his knowledge of lending practices was second to none, Edward had allowed his frustration to affect his willingness to help train and develop new hires in the department. This unsportsmanlike conduct had placed his prospects for promotion on indefinite hold.

The last thing he needed was to have someone like Alice waltz into his department and steal another management position away from him. Unbeknownst to Alice, Edward had accumulated a considerable following of his own among members of the senior management group. This support had been garnered through his participation in a number of key loan decisions involving their customers. His willingness to give their customers the benefit of the doubt on loan applications had helped him accumulate the sort of favored status that he could count on using to his own advantage.

As soon as Edward learned about Alice's interest in the credit management position, he wasted no time trying to stop her. What followed was a series of phone calls from himself to his executive following. The message that he sent was clear. If the executives weren't careful, they were going to find Alice and her new set of lending criteria governing all future loan decisions. Just to make sure they had no second thoughts, he tossed in a few false allegations against her. He insinuated that several of her acquisitions had lost money due to insufficient scrutiny on her part. He also implied that her evaluation methods were designed to get a lot of acquisitions done in a hurry, and were therefore suspect. While the things he said weren't entirely true, the message the executives got was abundantly clear. If Alice the amateur was allowed to eclipse Edward the expert, it meant no more Mr. Nice Guy helping them push their loans through. Presented with this cockamamie story about Alice, the decisionmakers were more than willing to conclude what all politicians conclude when they have ulterior motives at stake:

IT'S TRUE ! -- MORAL LESS

In the end, Alice finally ended up becoming the Senior Credit Manager - for a different company. In retrospect, it may have seemed to her and those around her that the attack on her was personal.

Not so.

Her story is a living embodiment of one of the most time-honored truths in politics.

"Politics is never about people. It is **always** about control."

In politics, people aren't important if they can't be controlled. If they can't be controlled, they have to be circumvented by every means available, or failing that, eliminated by any means necessary.

History is full of examples of those who were pushed aside due to a lack of allegiance to the "power behind the throne". The political world has always had little tolerance for mavericks. The secret to success in politics is knowing where the real power lies, understanding how it operates and sticking close to it at all times. There is a big difference between those who abide by these truths and those who do not.

Those who do remain contenders for higher office.

Those who do not end up...

BEYOND A REASONABLE CLOUT

Like it or not, in every company there is a political spectrum. At one end are those who are undeniably in control of everything that happens on a day-to-day basis. At the opposite end are those who have no influence whatsoever. For most corporate career-seekers, there is an unfortunate truth they have to live with...

There are a whole lot more slots available at the insignificant end of the spectrum than there are at the other.

In a clan environment, this imbalance in opportunities tips the scale in favor of those less burdened with concern for the welfare of their fellow man. Like hyenas whose newborn offspring will fight to the death for the chance of becoming top dog, there are predators in the corporate world who won't hesitate to have their colleagues for lunch if it presents an opportunity to get ahead. In their case, they don't just discredit someone to keep them from getting ahead. They drive them out altogether.

It represents the most extreme form of political behavior. Indiscriminately used, it has the potential to ruin more than a victim's prospects for employment. It can destroy their self-esteem, their relationships and even their livelihood.

The destruction can be served up in one of two ways. The first involves the use of unprovoked, pre-emptive strikes. The second is a bit more subtle. It involves the use of steadily applied pressure to help the victim self-destruct.

The pre-emptive variety is delivered by those whose desire to get ahead is exceeded only by their ability. These people are formidable adversaries because they have both the know-how and the killer instinct to get ahead. The only thing they lack is tolerance for any form of competition.

When you cross paths with one of these prima donnas, it's only a matter of time before you're counting the tread marks across your back. At least that's what Jack learned when he had the total misfortune to experience first-hand what it's like to live in the nightmare world of...

MALICE IN WUNDERKIND

Jack was a Regional Sales Director for a national distributor of construction materials. In this position, he was one of three Directors who were each responsible for a different territory in the continental U.S. Of the other two directors, one had held the position for more than three years. The other, whose name was Bruce, had recently been promoted to the post after a short stint as Sales Manager for one of the local field offices. In less than four years, Bruce had been promoted four times from an entry level sales position to Regional Sales Director. All that remained between Bruce and the President's office were the positions of Vice President of Sales, Senior Vice President of Operations and Chief Operating Officer.

At first, Jack and the other director were a bit wary of this newcomer to their ranks. The startling amount of success which Bruce had achieved in such a short time was unsettling at first. There were, after all, some rumors circulating about Bruce's lack of team play. Even more troublesome were the whispered accusations about questionable conduct involving former peers. However, as time went by, Bruce managed to warm up to them by regularly seeking their counsel. He was particularly deferential to Jack. They would regularly have lunch together to exchange ideas and swap horror stories. Bruce was constantly picking Jack's brain for information. Which were Jack's best territories? Which managers were his weakest? How was he dealing with them? After a while, it seemed to Jack that Bruce was really an OK guy who was genuinely interested in the success of the business, and did not deserve his reputation for being heavy-handed with subordinates and opportunistic with superiors.

And he kept right on believing that until the day he learned that his territory was being reduced. The explanation given was a prolonged failure to deal more swiftly with underperforming managers in his territories. The Vice President of Sales was now demanding remedial action immediately.

And Bruce was just the man for the job.

Bruce had managed to impress his boss with his early grasp of the situation in Jack's territory as well as his own. He seemed to have extraordinary insight into the cause of these shortcomings. Above all, Bruce showed the sort of impatience with underperformance that his boss wanted put to use on a larger scale. Consequently, Jack found himself relieved of almost half his territory... all of which was turned over to Bruce.

Needless to say, Jack was a little upset with this turn of events. This was the first realignment of territory to ever take place, and he had come up on the short end of it. Suspecting that Bruce had used their relationship to take unfair advantage of the situation, he confronted Bruce about it the following day. The conversation went something like this:

Jack: "Would you like to tell me how our boss came to the sudden realization that you were the answer to all of our problems?"

Bruce: "Consider yourself fortunate that you have any territory left. It's only a matter of time before you're out of here."

Jack's tale, while an especially bitter one, is not overly unusual when wunderkind are unleashed upon the mere mortals in corporate society. Yet, not every organization has these wunderkind to wreak havoc on its rank and file. In their absence, the corporate playing field is more level for everyone else. However, even when the playing field is level for everyone involved, there can still be problems. When members of a society of equals set out to distinguish themselves as the one and only choice for a leadership position, some will seek an unfair advantage. When that happens, an otherwise smooth-sailing organization can wind up in...

THE ONE-UPSMANSHIP-WRECK

Any number of situations can lend themselves to this sort of mayhem. The textbook variety takes place immediately following the merger of two firms. Mergers and acquisitions have a nasty habit of pitting two or more people against each other for a single position. After all, no organization needs two tax managers, two planning managers, two chief accountants or two directors of human resources. The maneuvering can get quite political when the situation calls for one person to remain in charge and the other to be outplaced. The business journals are packed with stories about leaders of newly combined companies who failed to act quickly and decisively to head off resultant infighting between rivals, leaving in their wake many confused employees and concerned shareholders.

However, it doesn't always take a merger with another company to start the wrecking ball rolling. Sometimes, there can be contention between managers who are responsible for different aspects of the same business. A lot of companies unwittingly institutionalize this sort of rivalry by segmenting their management structure. The most typical examples of this segmentation are organizations that have one set of managers in charge of existing business operations and another in charge of new business initiatives. New business initiatives include things such as acquisitions, new product development and strategic business alliances and partnerships with other companies. They represent investments in the future of the organization and are generally viewed as an indispensable part of the business.

So how can something so germane to the business generate so much political infighting?

By nature, new business activities tend to be high-yield, low-probable events. That means they pay huge dividends in those rare situations where they pay anything at all. They usually end up consuming vast amounts of time and money. The hard lessons they teach are often the only thing of value to be taken away from these ventures. Given their somewhat limited prospects, some new business managers succumb to the urge to paint a rosier picture of these prospects than the facts can support. The logic behind it is simple. If, through clever maneuvering or posturing, they can make a low-probable event appear high-probable, they can make a high-dollar outcome seem inevitable. There are some new business executives who have perfected this technique, as evidenced by this oft-repeated scenario:

Official Announcement from the New Business Department:
"Interest in the new product has been building rapidly. Expressions of interest have been made by several major customers and our survey

shows that three out of five respondents would be willing to purchase it at or near the proposed price point."

Actual Translation
"A heck of a lot of time and money has already been used up on this idea. It's a pity we didn't do enough market research on the front end to see how tough it would be to sell the bloody thing. For every customer we manage to convince to take a look at it, another two decide they don't need it. We're now prepared to offer it at a discount or turn it into a loss leader if that's what it will take to recover some of the investment."

The intent of this ploy is fairly straightforward. Like any other political maneuver, the goal is to gain the upper hand and to shift momentum away from those who might have a more legitimate claim on the attention of top management. Why does it succeed so often? It succeeds because it harnesses one of the greatest powers present in the modern-day business world. It's known as...

THE SHINING

In this Stephen King novel, the central characters displayed a supernatural ability to project their own thoughts and feelings into the minds of others. This surrealistic ability is currently shared by the political constituents of the business world. And the effect can be just as eerie.

The shining is an irresistible force that works its way into the inner recesses of the human brain. The same force is frequently used to sell apples and automobiles. Snow White, a somewhat innocent but by no means ignorant person, chose to eat a poisoned apple because it was the shiniest one the Wicked Queen had to offer. Automobiles can be sold to the equally innocent and occasionally ignorant for much more than they're worth if they also have a good shine on them. In the business world, ideas are constantly bought and sold based on how lustrous they look on the surface. As was true in the case of Snow

White, the shinier they appear, the more reason to fear. It is certainly not unusual to see a new business idea sold more on its promises than its merits - simply because nothing with such surface glitter can be found anywhere else in the company's existing business operations. Before long, a company's leadership can find itself spending more time gazing after what's new and different than on what it already knows is crucial. When the "what is already crucial" happens to generate the vast majority of the profit, that sort of neglect can prove very costly.

And who benefits from all this attention? It's the glitter guys and gals. They're the ones who devote all their time to coming up with new ideas. They're the ones who get the opportunity to consult with outsiders about the latest ideas and trends in their industry. They're the ones who get to spend the most time presenting to senior management. The resources that go along with all of that recognition can easily shift the momentum of an entire organization. Those who use this unfair advantage to get ahead of their peers can continually position their ideas in a way that allows them to steal the spotlight from other, more worthy undertakings. The resulting transfer of energy out of the company's main line of business can often prove irreversible, especially when it becomes too obvious to too many that the company's main line is no longer the right line to stand in.

CHAPTER SUMMARY

If packs are known for their intimidators, and colonies for their manipulators, then clans are known for their instigators. Unlike their counterparts, whose politics stem predominantly from the leadership of the organization, clans generate their politics at the grass roots level.

Clan politics are the outgrowth of a dog-eat-dog environment where the rank and file are encouraged by a standoffish leadership group to battle each other for the chance to reach the ranks of top management. The competitive behavior it encourages includes a variety of heavy-handed and under-handed tactics that rivals use to beat their opponents. The categories range from the totally clandestine to the openly hostile.

As the behavior moves from one extreme to the other, so does the number of combatants. At the low end, you find the *hush-hush sweet charlatan* approach, whereby the aggressor secretly pretends to be the best friend their victim ever had - for as long as it takes to learn their weaknesses and bushwhack them. Next up the scale is a more antagonistic form of behavior whereby the assailant goes on a *quest for fire-ing* that continues until the victim is finally forced out of the organization. When both the predator and the prey stem from the management ranks of the organization, there is nothing to stop either one from using anyone or anything at their disposal to see the loser sitting *pretty in pink-slip*.

When this ruthless behavior moves beyond one-on-one skirmishes to two or more against one, even the most senior of executives can be forced to walk the plank by roving *pirates of pensions*. By virtue of their strength in numbers, the rank and file can occasionally pick off some of their slower moving chieftains who venture too far from the shelter of the executive suite. Sometimes the victim will walk right into it by carelessly divulging some innocent mistake they made. Politicians definitely use that to their full advantage, forcing the hapless truth-teller to pay *the high price of admission*. It tells others in the organization who have a similar tendency to bare their souls to think twice before doing so. That's because when *your slip-up is showing*, most people won't say or do anything until it is too late. Unsafe admissions enable adversaries to permanently park an opponent's career. Careless confessions can also be used by sibling rivals to lure their prey into *the parent company trap*, from which there is little hope of escape.

With each victim's demise comes another opportunity for someone to advance. Depending on the position at stake, the battle can escalate to the point where entire departments and divisions of a company will engage each other. *The way we war* depends on the amount of love lost between the two factions. If the two sides have always been enemies, the level of *raging bull* _ _ _ _ will be considerable. Hostile words and actions will be traded back and forth with the same speed and intensity you'd find on the floor of a stock exchange. Meanwhile, the morale of the troops diminishes the longer the conflict is allowed to continue. After a certain point, it makes little difference who is the victor and who is the vanquished. The business suffers so much that all anyone can see when it's over is *how the worst was won*. The lasting injuries inflicted by both sides during their war of words and deeds will often cause a widespread *staff infection* that can seriously jeopardize the future health and well being of the entire organization.

The worst casualties from this warfare are those suffered by customers. At the onset of hostilities, neither side tries very hard to protect these innocent bystanders. Customers find themselves with service that has either been boycotted or sabotaged. Since they have nothing at all to gain from the conflict, they promptly emigrate to another company where their needs and expectations will be met with enthusiasm instead of hostility.

Unfortunately, the mark of a brave warrior is the ability to set aside casualties and continue the fight. So it goes in corporate politics. Those with something to gain will continue to lead their subordinates on. However, the embattled employees start to question their own involvement. The need for reinforcement causes them to band together into cliques in order to restore the sense of unity, purpose and self-confidence that they lost during the extended fighting. Once these smaller factions have time to coalesce, they start pursuing their own separate agendas. When those agendas call for someone to be "downsized", these cliques will band together to form a *discredit union* to assault their opponent. Using whatever devious means necessary, they launch a campaign of deception involving a lot of *talking on the tell-a-phony line*. It doesn't matter to them how underhanded it gets. As long as enough people can be convinced to accept fabrications as the gospel truth, then as far as they're concerned, *it's true - moral less*.

While this sort of vindictive behavior is surprising and appalling to the casual observer, for insiders it is an accepted way of life in the world of corporate politics. What insiders understand and outsiders don't is the fact that in their world, a person will end up in one of two places - either beyond the reach of his former peers in the upper ranks of management, or *beyond a reasonable clout*. To escape the dubious fate in the latter category, combatants will use everything at their disposal to win the day. If they happen to be gifted with exceptional talent, one can expect to see a showing of *malice in wunderkind* as those gifts are used against the opposition. Those who aren't exceptionally gifted are forced to find other ways to compete. Many resort to using their position as a weapon, particularly if it's the kind that affords them regular contact with higher-ups in the organization. As more and more management time is squandered on issues raised by warring factions, the day-to-day business suffers. As the company's vision becomes more and more clouded, the organization becomes a drifting boat seeking guidance from the nearest lighthouse. Unfortunately, most end up sailing into a *one-upsmanship-wreck* because they were diverted from the lighthouse by *the shining* of a fabulous new business opportunity. Blinded by the gleam of a get-richer-quick scheme, they steer the organization off its original course in search of the proverbial pot of gold at the end of the rainbow. When the gold doesn't pan out, it becomes even more difficult for the organization to get back on course again.

The helpless, hollowed out feeling this leaves behind in the workforce is far more debilitating than anything the organization's competitors could hope for. With employees and customers in a highly dissatisfied state, the prospects for a successful turnaround diminish rapidly.

The leadership, whose unwillingness to interact with employees and customers adds insult to this injury, promptly go from being polarized to paralyzed. Until the arrival of new leadership breaks through this self-inflicted inertia, precious momentum is allowed to slip away.

CHAPTER 6

FLOATING WITH THE POD

Animals that travel together in pods have a much more highly developed sense of community. They live and work together in harmony, focusing on the protection and development of their younger members. Everyone is generally treated as an equal and there are no overt attempts made to dominate any of the other members.

You'll never find anyone in this group at cross-porpoises.

Despite their selfless nature, they are extremely cunning and ferocious. The dolphins and killer whales who are part of this group are very successful hunters. They have a keenly developed sense of sonar that they use to locate what they're after. They can attack and overcome adversaries or prey that are considerably larger in size.

In the corporate world, you're part of a pod if both the leaders and the followers are mutually supportive. Their highly desirable traits include:

Leaders who are selfless in nature.
Leaders who consider and treat followers as equals.
Followers who are focused on the best interests of the group.
Followers who act as leaders when called upon to do so.

There are hundreds of ways to describe how antithetical the typical corporate bureaucracy is to this group. One of the best can be found in a recent book about Southwest Airlines. In this in-depth study of one of American business' biggest success stories, authors Kevin and Jackie Freiberg relay the views of Herb Kelleher, Southwest's Chairman and CEO, about how excessive corporate bureaucracy "...results from the egos of empire builders who try, through title and position, to emphasize their own importance."[2]

Unfortunately, the number of companies in this best-of-the-four categories is very small indeed. While no organization is immune to politics, those in this category possess the unique ability to minimize it by doing two things exceptionally well:

1. They keep their business structure, systems and procedures simple.

2. They understand the importance of doing *every* job *very* well.

At the risk of oversimplifying, you can look at the parts of an organization the same way you would the moving parts on a car.

Steering Mechanism- Management
Powertrain - Products and services
Wheel Assembly - Offices and branches
Tires - Employees

Why are employees relegated to the seemingly insignificant status of tires?

It makes perfect sense when you consider the following:

---

[2] Kevin & Jackie Freiberg, <u>Nuts! Southwest Airlines' Crazy Recipe for Business and Personal Success</u> (New York: Broadway Books, 1996) 76.

Which of those parts makes continuous contact with the outside world?

Which of those parts is the most frequently changed out?

Which of those parts gets kicked when a buyer shows up?

If you recently acquired a new or used car, chances are you didn't buy it because you liked the tires. The same holds true for organizations. Buyers want them because they like how the steering (management) handles, and how fast the engine (product and service) goes. The tires never get a second thought... unless of course they're attached to a pod. Pod-like people, like those you find at Southwest Airlines, understand the importance of keeping a very satisfied and well trained workforce in constant contact with their customers. Towards that end, the principals in the firm make it a point to cultivate a supportive working environment where people in different positions each receive an equal amount of recognition.

Just in case you have doubts, you should know that one thousand dollars of Southwest Airlines stock back in 1973 is now worth more than one million dollars today. All that in an industry that lost $12.8 billion between 1990 and 1994, more money than it made in the previous 60 years! [3]

It all works when you follow the rules in **Dis'n De'**ng order.

Dis-tinguished efforts from **De**-voted employees
prevents
Dis-service to **De**-valued customers

---

[3] Kevin & Jackie Freiberg, Nuts! Southwest Airlines' Crazy Recipe for Business and Personal Success (New York: Broadway Books, 1996) 4-5.

CONCLUSION

IT'S TIME TO CHANGE YOUR UNAWARE

Suffice it to say that politics comes in many forms. It is resident in virtually every organization, regardless of shape and size.

Politics comes into play when one of the many elements of a society, government or organization either fails to do its own job, or tries to do somebody else's job, or both. When people fail to do the job they are charged with, it's because they're either not sure what it is, they're not sure how to do it, or they'd rather be doing something else. The imbalances that these failures create are an everyday fact of life in most organizations. The conflicts that ensue as the organization struggles to regain its balance often escalate into costly power struggles.

Responding to the imbalance created by the neglect or failure of others, the political elements try to correct the situation in a way that serves their own best interests. But behavior that is self-indulgent keeps the organization off-center. Like a washing machine with an imbalanced load, it continues to spin out of control, knocking itself out of kilter, wandering aimlessly about until the cycle ends.

Unfortunately, for most organizations, this vicious cycle never seems to end. That is because most people in the organization do not know how to deal with political behavior. It confuses them. It confounds them. It knocks *them* off-balance. In this disoriented condition, people typically make one of five major mistakes - mistakes which hasten the spread of politics throughout the organization.

1. They deny its existence. They cope with the situation by refusing to acknowledge it altogether.

2. They adapt to it. They talk themselves into believing it has no harmful long term side-effects.

3. They legitimize it by rallying behind those who practice it.

4. They exhaust themselves struggling against it, and constantly worrying or complaining about it.

5. They try to escape it. They jump from one organization to another hoping that the politics will be less prevalent the next time around.

Those who resort to the escape route discover all too quickly that escape is virtually impossible. They learn the hard way that corporate politics is like VISA ⁴...

"It's everywhere you want to be."

Faced with this reality, many are now choosing to avoid or escape organizational life altogether.

While going into business for yourself and becoming your own boss can be very rewarding, it is also very difficult. Only those who possess all of the mental, physical, personal and financial resources necessary to take that escape route are in the best position to try for it.

---

⁴ VISA is a registered trademark of VISA USA.

While entrepreneurship is definitely on the rise in the U.S., there are many who still prefer the structure and sense of community that organizations have to offer. People by nature are gregarious. Their inclination is to become a part of something larger and accomplish some greater purpose. The sense of togetherness not only helps accomplish the goal, it makes the process a lot more meaningful for everyone involved.

When you understand the importance of these associations to most people, you cannot expect them to risk everything in some reckless attempt to escape the politics of corporate life. Despite the recent swell in entrepreneurial spirit, there are still a lot of organizations and people out there who need each other to succeed. The trick is finding appropriate ways to coexist with the corporate politics that is inevitably bred when people and organizations come together.

It is very possible for a person to find contentment, even fulfillment in an organization that is rife with politics. Knowing how to find real meaning in that sort of environment can, in the long run, be a lot more gratifying than indulging the urge to escape. The old saying about the finest metal being forged in the hottest furnace holds true in this case. If one is able to come to grips with the political forces at work in their environment, it strengthens their resolve. It increases their flexibility and helps them realize their full potential. It can actually open up new opportunities for them.

The secret is to focus your attention on those aspects of the working environment that you can better understand, learn from, and ultimately influence. Your guiding principle should read like the prayer of Saint Francis.

"God, Grant me the serenity to accept the things I cannot change, the courage to change the things I can, and the wisdom to know the difference."

To better understand the importance of this mindset, let's borrow once again from the example of Southwest Airlines. As we saw in the previous chapter, Southwest has adopted a very unique and highly successful approach towards their employees and customers. One of the best ways to illustrate how well it works is to think of the journey that people make with their organizations as being analogous to a commercial airline flight. The similarities are really quite intriguing, starting with the cast of characters:

	Commercial Flight	Commercial Enterprise
Each has on board	Passengers	Employees
The leader is the	Pilot	CEO
Next in charge is the	Co-Pilot	COO
Supported by the	Flight Crew	Executive Officers
And overseen by the	Ground Control	Board of Directors

What about the customers? Aren't customers a rather important part of a commercial flight or commercial enterprise?

Yes they are. But the customers of a commercial airline are not the people who fly as passengers on the aircraft. The customers are the people who depend on the airline to deliver their friends, associates and loved ones to them safe and sound. The customers of a commercial business depend upon the organization to deliver to them a satisfied bunch of employees with all of the energies and skills necessary to help give them what they want - all day, every day. When you think of it in those terms, it's just as important for a business to take care of its employees as it is for an airline to take care of its passengers.

The airplane analogy is the basic conceptual model for most business organizations. What makes things complicated is when business and politics come together to create turbulence on the inside. It's bad enough that companies have to deal with frequent and unexpected turbulence from the outside. Having to deal with it on the inside makes life all the more difficult.

To better illustrate that point, take one more light-hearted look at the types of politics whose turbulence you're likely to encounter during your flight.

<u>Sure signs that the flight you're on is **PACK**ed with politics</u>:

1. There's a big sign in bold letters on the cockpit door that reads..

"LEAVE THE DRIVING TO US...OR ELSE"

2. The pilots frequently leave the cockpit to yell at the flight crew.

3. The flight crew frequently visits the main cabin to yell at the passengers.

4. The passengers apologize to the crew for making the crew mad, and either take it out on each other or the people waiting for them at the gate.

<u>Sure signs that you're flying on **COLONY**-all Airways</u>

1. The pilot and co-pilot are constantly battling each other for control of the aircraft. Meanwhile, they are asking the flight attendants for tips on how to fly the plane.

2. The flight attendants are constantly informing the coach passengers how much nicer it is in first class.

3. The passengers are constantly tripping over themselves to help the flight crew do their job.

4. After the flight, friends and relatives at the gate are forced to wait because the passengers can't bring themselves to leave the plane.

<u>Tips that you're on an aircraft that's reducing speed and altitude in order to **C - LAN'd**</u>

1. The pilots have no idea who their flight crew is, and could care less.

2. The flight attendants spend all their time with their ears pressed to the cockpit door trying to figure out what's going to happen next.

3. The passengers try to steal the seats in front of them whenever the occupants get up to go to the restroom.

4. No one is waiting for the plane at the gate because it arrived at the wrong gate.

When you view corporate politics from this perspective, you start to get some idea why airplanes are almost always successful at getting where they're going and most organizations are not.

Organizations frequently fly off course because the people aboard them lose sight of something very critical to success... *their responsibility to their position*.

On airplanes and in organizations, everyone has a position. *Every position has a responsibility for something and/or someone*. Pilots and crew members, just like chief executives and managers, have different positions with different responsibilities for different things and different people. What makes the airplane crew more successful is the way in which they carry out their responsibilities.

Crew members on an airplane perform their jobs by paying specific attention to their position and their place on the aircraft. Their positions obligate them to certain people and specific tasks.

The pilots, who have the ultimate responsibility for the safety of the aircraft and everyone aboard, confine themselves to the cockpit where they possess the ways and means to carry out that responsibility.

The navigator, who has responsibility for keeping the aircraft on course, remains in the cockpit where (s)he can help guide the plane.

The cabin crew, who are responsible for the well-being of the passengers, remain in the cabin area where they can pay attention to the needs of the passengers.

The people in the control tower, who remain stationed on the ground, are responsible for directing and tracking it throughout its flight.

Imagine what would happen if the crew members on an airplane decided to do something other than what their position demanded.

What would happen, for example, if the pilot were to routinely venture out of the cockpit to help the flight attendants serve drinks?

What if the co-pilot insisted on instructing the control tower how to direct other air traffic?

What if the flight attendants decided to barge into the cockpit every fifteen minutes to demand a flight status report?

What would happen if the tower requested the plane to make an unscheduled stop so that one of their controllers could inspect it?

What would happen if the passengers were allowed, even encouraged to fight each other for the best seats on the airplane?

By now I'm sure you get the idea.

Politics is all about people trying to do something or be something beyond what their position demands of them.

Organizations, like aircraft, have only one pilot (chief executive officer). Depending on its size, it may also have a co-pilot (chief operating officer). The cockpit (corner office) is restricted to the pilots (chief executives) who have the final responsibility for safeguarding the aircraft (organization) and protecting the welfare of the passengers (employees).

From a business standpoint, the cockpit symbolizes a place reserved for those whose vision requires that they have a full and unobstructed view of where they are taking the organization. In business, that responsibility falls to the CEO.

Now consider what would happen if the CEO were to concern himself (herself) with the happiness of everyone on board the organization. Instead of leaving that responsibility to the crew working outside the corner office, let's say for example that the CEO insisted on handling that responsibility themselves.

Sounds legitimate, doesn't it? In fact, you've read plenty of articles about chief executives who insisted that their open door policy made it possible for them to readily identify the concerns of employees and intervene directly on their behalf.

Now picture for a moment what would happen if a commercial airline pilot decided to have an open cockpit door policy for everyone on the aircraft. At the risk of over-emphasizing the point, there is a big difference between protecting the welfare of passengers and ensuring their happiness. A pilot's primary concern is their welfare, not their happiness. Happiness is the responsibility of the rest of the flight crew who work outside the cockpit.

If necessary, a pilot will stand a plane on its nose if necessary to protect the lives of the passengers. To a pilot's way of thinking, the passengers are better off scared than dead.

Not so in the business world. When business leaders are faced with emergency situations, and are overwhelmed by the pressure for more results, they often divert themselves by meddling with the people and systems they believe are at fault. As leaders instinctively bow to these pressures, they become habitual offenders, constantly intervening at the first sign of trouble.

On a theoretical level, this sort of frequent intervention appears to be the act of a closely connected, highly responsive leader with a very well developed knack for problem solving.

On a practical level, it is a formula for disaster.

When a chief executive, or any other employee for that matter, digresses from the unique responsibilities of their position to shore up those belonging to someone else, they neglect their obligations to the people and tasks that only they are equipped to deal with.

For example:

A company's board of directors cannot refuse to replace a chief executive with a penchant for making excuses because they are afraid of the impact it will have on the stock price.

Chief executive officers cannot neglect their responsibility for defining and articulating a much-needed corporate strategy because they feel more comfortable with a simple restructuring.

Chief operating officers cannot neglect their responsibility for operating performance, procedures and policies in order to focus exclusively on new lines of business.

Chief financial officers cannot neglect their responsibility for reporting on the condition of the company because they would rather concentrate on acquisitions.

Chief information officers cannot abandon their obligation to produce accurate, relevant and timely data in order to pursue the latest technology.

If you do happen to find yourself in the midst of a politically-charged organization where everyone is apparently trying to do someone else's job, you have some very important decisions to make.

The most critical one is...

SHOULD I BAIL OUT?

The first simple rule in this regard is to never bail out as a reflex action. The prospect of enduring turbulence or a rough landing is far better than the feeling you get if you suddenly find yourself in freefall, waiting helplessly to hit bottom.

If you think that leaving well is the best revenge, you need two things:

1. A good reason.
2. A good parachute.

There are plenty of different opinions about what constitutes a good reason. Going back to the airplane analogy, let's start by defining what a good reason is *not*.

A good reason is *not* because you personally dislike the pilot, co-pilot, flight crew or other passengers (unless of course it's due to harassment).

A good reason is *not* because you hate turbulence.

A good reason is *not* because you can't sit in your favorite seat.

A good reason *is* because you've seen the flight plan, and you know the company is going to land in the wrong place (or in the wrong hands).

A good reason *is* because you've seen the maintenance log, and you're convinced the company is no longer airworthy.

Assuming your reason for bailing out is a good one, the next thing you need to know is what kind of parachute you have. (You can worry about what color it is later). It's important because, in this modern world of ours, the act of bailing out is no longer what it used to be. Nowadays, you can't be sure that your next flight will be any longer or any smoother than the last one.

So before you bail, heed this without fail.

1. If there isn't another job already waiting for you, make sure the financial resources you take with you are enough to let you down gently. You never know how long your next flight will be delayed.

2. If you've managed to book your next flight, make sure there's a good connection. Otherwise the next leg of your journey may terminate sooner than you think.

What should you do if you don't have a good reason and a good parachute?

You have two choices.

1. You can either be completely lost, confused and angered by the politics in your organization.

Or...

2. You can peacefully co-exist with the chaos, and marvel at the workings of this unshakable reality of the business world.

The first choice is the instinctive one for most people. People in organizations have a tendency to panic when they sense that their personal career path and the organization's flight path are no longer in sync. The harder they try to superimpose their own personal flight plan on top of the organization's, the more they get rebuffed. The constant frustration causes them to become angry and fearful. It has been well documented that when the mind is dominated by fear, anxiety, or self-preoccupation, the world tends to appear hostile or threatening.[5] In this condition, people start to indulge in a variety of self-protective behaviors that eventually leave themselves and the organization even more vulnerable to the spread of politics.

For those who are upset by wanton displays of power politics, it's important to understand that in the business world, power is like energy. It is neither created or destroyed. The power that is distributed across the corporate landscape is like the distribution of wealth across America; it is uneven. Nevertheless, each person in a position of responsibility - from the mail room up to the board room - shares some portion of this power. The formula that determines how the power is distributed is really quite simple.

The amount of power people possess = the amount they need to carry out the responsibilities of their position.

Corporate politics is all about this balance of power, which explains why it is so prevalent. When people assemble to work towards a common goal, there are always those who want more power than their position affords them. These people are known as "grabbers". At the opposite end are those who prefer less responsibility than their position demands. These are known as "abdicators". In between are a whole host of people bartering power back and forth as their situation demands. These are known as "traders".

When people think about corporate politics, they tend to view it as a function of the grabbers and their insatiable appetite for more power.

That's not completely accurate.

---

[5] Joel Levey and Michelle Levey, <u>Living in Balance</u> (Berkeley, CA: Conari Press, 1998) .

It always takes two to tango. In this case, the abdicators are as much a contributor to corporate politics as anyone else. Whenever these people knowingly or unknowingly abdicate one or more responsibilities of their position, they cause a shift in the balance of power. By giving up control over their own situation, they allow others to seize it for their own benefit. More often than not, the ones who seize it are the ones who are always in the market for it, namely the grabbers. Once they seize it, they are then free to use it against those who relinquished it.

Those who choose to respond to a political environment in this fashion, by withdrawing or blindly striking out against it, actually end up accomplishing the exact opposite outcome. Instead of impeding its growth, their behavior serves to advance the spread of politics throughout the organization.

Fortunately, there is another way to respond that is a more challenging, and potentially rewarding one. It requires one to acknowledge that politics and business are destined to coexist whenever people come together to work towards a common goal. It helps provide a balanced perspective about corporate politics and the people who practice it.

In his analysis of the rise and fall of twenty civilizations, the great historian Arnold Toynbee offers some insight into the importance of balance. In the Law of Progressive Simplification which he formulated, it states that the growth and vitality of a civilization is not a function of power over land or power over people. Rather, the measure of a civilization's growth is in its ability to transfer increasing amounts of energy and attention from the material side of life to the psychological, cultural, aesthetic and spiritual side of life.[6]

---

[6] Joel Levey and Michelle Levey, <u>Living in Balance</u> (Berkeley, CA: Conari Press, 1998).

Within the context of a business organization, this Law suggests that, whenever possible, you should direct your attention away from the politics raging alongside of you and instead focus on fulfilling the higher obligations of your own position. It doesn't mean you fulfill only those obligations that suit you. It means you fulfill every single one of them. That includes meeting the needs of those who depend on your position for help in serving the organization, its employees and its customers.

By faithfully carrying out the full measure of your responsibilities, you hold on to the power that is legitimately yours. By refraining from grabbing power that you don't need, or abdicating power that you do need, you contribute to a much-needed sense of balance, not only for yourself, but for your organization as well.

To be continued...

AFTERWORD

It is my sincere hope that this writing had a positive impact on you.

Whether it helped recollect a memory, raise an issue or strike a nerve is of very great importance to me.

The world of corporate politics wasn't always as familiar to me as it is now. I hope it is now more familiar to you.

If you have a story to tell about your own experience with corporate politics, I would like to hear from you. Please send us your story via our e-mail address at

stories@thetruthsquad.com

If possible, any attachments should be sent in a current version of Microsoft Word.

For more information about the book, the author or The Truth Squad, please contact us at our website

www.thetruthsquad.com

Here's wishing you the best of luck in all of your future endeavors.

Printed in the United States
34493LVS00001B/137